POWER UP!

Other Kaplan Power Books:

Kaplan Learning Power
Kaplan Math Power
Kaplan Word Power
Kaplan Writing Power

Other Kaplan Writing Books:

SAT II: Writing
Yale Daily News Guide to Writing College Papers

WRITING POWER

THIRD EDITION

by Nancy White

Simon & Schuster

NEW YORK · LONDON · SINGAPORE · SYDNEY · TORONTO

Kaplan Publishing
Published by Simon & Schuster
1230 Avenue of the Americas
New York, NY 10020

For bulk sales to schools, colleges, and universities, please contact Order Department, Simon & Schuster, 100 Front Street, Riverside, NJ 08075. Phone: 1-800-223-2336. Fax: 1-800-943-9831.

Contributing Editors: Seppy Basili and Trent Anderson
Project Editor: Megan Duffy
Interior Page Production: Laurel Douglas and Jan Gladish
Production Manager: Michael Shevlin
Production Editor: Maude Spekes
Cover Design: Cheung Tai
Editorial Coordinator: Déa Alessandro
Executive Editor: Del Franz

Manufactured in the United States of America
Published simultaneously in Canada

March 2003
10 9 8 7 6 5 4 3 2 1

ISBN 0-7432-4116-9

TABLE OF CONTENTS

KAPLAN

ABOUT THE AUTHOR

First a teacher of English and creative writing, then an educational publishing executive in New York, Nancy White has overseen projects from pre-school language arts to college chemistry. Her most recent project (before *Writing Power*) was a series of writing guides for middle-school students. She is the author of numerous books for young people, including *The Kids' Science Book* and *Why Do Dogs Do That?*

The Power of *Writing Power*

WHAT IS "WRITING POWER"?

Quite simply, writing power is having a writing system—one that works. Most good writers use some version of this system, whether consciously or intuitively. Now you will be able to use it, too.

If having a writing system is completely new to you, don't worry. We will talk you through it, step by step. Then we will show you how to apply it to different types of writing, from college-application essays to reports. You may find that you have already been using *Writing Power,* perhaps without even realizing it. If so, this book will help you learn to use it even better.

You may be fine once you get started, but agonize over getting those first few sentences down on paper. Or perhaps you zip through your first draft but have trouble polishing your final copy. In either case, you can use *Writing Power* to focus on specific areas where you are having trouble.

Finally, you may feel confident as a writer of one kind of material but are not sure how to apply your skills to complete a particular task at work or school. *Writing Power* will help you master the kind of writing you are unsure about, whether it is an essay for your SAT or a report to your boss about a new management plan. We will talk you through the do's and don'ts of the specific writing question. We will help you to understand what the purpose and style of your writing should be so that you can complete your tasks easily and effectively.

We will also show you how to connect with your own power as a writer. But first, we are going to share with you a writing secret that even some professional writers don't know.

WRITING: THE BEST KEPT SECRET

Okay, are you ready for writing's best-kept secret? The one that will change your attitude about writing forever? Here it is: Everyone worries about writing!

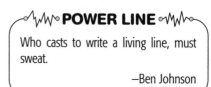

∿∿● **POWER LINE** ●∿∿

Who casts to write a living line, must sweat.

—Ben Johnson

That's right. Everyone who writes—even Nobel Prize–winning novelists—feels a sense of dread when confronted by a blank page. Everyone feels exposed. Everyone worries that he or she won't have anything to say, won't say it right, won't say it as well as someone else, won't say it at all. So the fact that you worry about writing doesn't mean that you're not a writer. It means that you are a writer. Join the club!

Now, here's the second best-kept secret about writing: Anyone can learn to do it well. It just takes practice.

Learning to write well is like learning any skill. Take driving: Remember when you first got behind the wheel? There were so many things to keep track of! How could you keep your eyes on the road *and* check the rearview mirror *and* switch on the headlights *and* check the speedometer *and* watch for traffic coming from that intersection to your right? It seemed impossible to do all those things at once and still keep your mind on getting where you wanted to go. And if you knew that there was parallel parking at the end of your journey, forget it! The anticipation of that alone was enough to give you "driver's block."

But then, eventually, you did learn to drive. Suddenly, instead of focusing on all the separate details, you were able make everything come together. You could relax, and maybe even enjoy the sights along the way.

What made the difference? Partly, it was just practice. After you had changed lanes a hundred or so times, it started to seem easy, even automatic.

Partly, too, the difference is in your own sense of mastery. You eventually came to believe you were a good driver.

Now, when you want to exit the freeway, you automatically change lanes. If there is a lot of traffic or a blinding rainstorm, you might have to work harder than usual. But you don't question whether you should ever have gotten into the car in the first place. You understand that you're facing a tough situation, and you draw on both your skill and your self-confidence to get you through.

You can do the same with writing. Even if sitting down to write feels like heading into a blizzard, you will often surprise yourself by enjoying the landscape once you have actually gotten your bearings and have started on your writing journey.

HOW TO USE THIS BOOK

This book is your travel guide to writing. It is here to help you learn the skill in general, about a particular aspect of writing, or about a particular type of writing. Use this book as you need it. You do not have to start at the beginning and work page by page. We have given you a detailed table of contents so that you can pick and choose the topics you need when you need them. We do suggest that everyone at least glance through the first and second sections— "Rules for Writing" and "Starting the Process"—because the pearls of wisdom on those pages apply to virtually every type of writing.

Every chapter ends with a section called "Plug In." This section gives you a chance to try out the aspect of writing you have been reading about. Don't think of these features as drills or quizzes designed to trap you or show you up. Rather, think of them as practice sessions. They simply let you see what you've learned and what you still need to work on. (Remember, too, that whatever you write for a "Plug In" is for your eyes only, so relax—you're safe with us!) In most cases, "Plug In" is a flawed model of the type of writing covered in the chapter. You will have a chance to correct the mistakes and then compare your work to our own corrected version. In other cases, "Plug In" is more of a self-help exercise (not a quiz!). If you are not happy with your own progress on the "Plug Ins" you might go back and take another look at the chapter.

The main purpose of *Writing Power* is to help you connect to your own power as a writer. Anyone who chooses to write is a writer. All you may need is to become familiar with the terrain, learn some "rules of the road," and become confident enough to get behind the wheel. Good luck—we hope you enjoy the trip!

SECTION ONE

Rules for Writing

Play by the Rules

Writing is often like running a race, or participating in an important event. You need to think about the stages of writing, and where writing fits in with your individual plans, strengths, and weaknesses. Before you dive in to the following chapters, here are some power tips for using what is in this section.

Warming Up. Look through the whole section quickly, paying special attention to the Plug In or introductory sections. Become aware of the style, the way the book is divided up, and how it might be of value for you.

Stretching. Focus on the sections you need to know more about. Skip the areas in which you are in good shape. You may wish to come back to some of these, but for now you are toned up in some areas, and need some extra stretching in others.

Working Out. Carefully read through the sections you need to use. Find a quiet place where you can concentrate, and give it some time and thought. Take some notes, and jot down further questions you might have.

Training. Now, try some of the Your Turn exercises and Plug In sections in the book. These are designed to give you an idea about how you are doing, whether or not you understand each section. If you find there are certain areas in which you are not doing as well, let them sit for a day, then go back and try again.

Sprint. Decide which sections you know quickly and do not have to repeat.

Marathon. Pay special attention to those sections highlighted by a lightbulb icon—these are important rules and tips to help you master key concepts.

Cooling Down. After you have worked in this way for a while, take time to relax and let yourself read a great mystery, watch TV, or walk the dog. You need time to decompress and let things sink in after you have been trying to master this material. Take the time! Eat chocolate, if that is what will help.

Personal Best. When you have done all the exercises and quizzes, when you have researched further in other resources and have toned up your abilities, go on to the next task at hand. You have done your best. Refer to this rules sections as you need to: If you get flabby in any area, the rules will always be there for you to refer to.

KEEP IT SIMPLE

We've often noticed that many people use long, wordy phrases in their writing. They would never think of speaking in such a way. Maybe they're insecure and feel that their writing sounds more official or important with more "big words" in it. Or maybe they're simply following the examples of others. There are certainly plenty of politicians, professors, and business people who use such language.

The irony is that while big words and clumsy phrases might make your writing sound more like a politician's speech, they won't make your ideas any clearer to your reader. Trying to sound "fancy" is the one mistake that can ruin any piece of writing, even if the ideas are fantastic.

> **POWER LINE**
>
> Word carpentry is like any other kind of carpentry: you must join your sentences smoothly.
>
> —Anatole France

KAPLAN

Your Turn

Which of the following writing samples is confusing and hard to follow? In which does the idea simply leap out at you?

> At this point in time, our major goal is to eliminate the need for excess verbiage and superfluous phrasing, so as to ensure communication of maximum effectiveness.

> Right now, let's concentrate on cutting out extra words, so that people can understand your writing.

Of course, sometimes the idea that you want to express is complicated. All the more reason, then, to make sure that your writing is as simple as possible. If your complex idea absolutely forces you to write a complicated sentence or use a "big word," fine. But be sure that the complications are there because you need them, not because you think they make your writing more impressive.

FOUR GOLDEN RULES

The principles of good writing can be summed up by four key rules:

1. Be concise—keep it short and simple.
2. Be forceful—take a stand.
3. Be correct—attend to details.
4. Be polished—attend to details.

The following chapters will elaborate on each of these rules.

CHAPTER ONE

Rule One: Be Concise

Which of these sayings do you like better?

> Being brief—that is, using just the right words and getting right to the point—is crucial, or all important, for the writer who intends to create clever, memorable prose.
>
> Brevity is the soul of wit.

All right, so maybe we can't all create time-honored proverbs. But we can all learn to be brief. Professional writers often must adhere to a specific limit on the number of words in a manuscript, determined by editors and based on the space available. Invariably, writers must cut out at least one treasured phrase, or even "butcher" a favorite passage altogether. But guess what? Almost always, the writing, pared down to the essentials, turns out to be even better in the briefer "bare bones" version.

And so, without further ado, here are four specific things to avoid that will help make your writing concise.

1. USE THE FEWEST WORDS POSSIBLE

Don't use several words when one will do. This is our golden rule: If you have the choice of saying something in one word or three words, always say it in one. Here are some examples of multiword phrases that can easily be pared down to a single syllable or two:

Wordy	Concise
at this point in time	now
at the present moment	now
at this very moment	now
immediately following	then
subsequent to	after
at a later time	later
prior to	before
in the days and weeks preceding	before

Get the idea? You can implement this suggestion in two ways. First, when you're writing, get used to reaching for the concise word rather than for the long-winded phrase. Second, when you look back at what you've written, keep an eye out for long, wordy phrases that you can replace with fewer, simpler words.

> ∿∿ **POWER LINE** ∿∿
>
> Look for clutter in your writing and prune it ruthlessly. Be grateful for everything you can throw away. Re-examine each sentence that you put on paper. Is every word doing new work? Can any thought be expressed with more economy? Is anything pompous or pretentious or faddish? Are you hanging on to something useless just because you think it's beautiful? Simplify. Simplify.
>
> –William Zinsser, *On Writing Well*

2. DON'T SAY IT AGAIN

Avoid redundancy, or needless repetition. Usually it occurs because writers say things that they don't even realize they've already said! For example,

> Our office is implementing a training program for beginners lacking experience.

Oh really? As opposed to all those experienced beginners? "Beginners lacking experience" is redundant. Here are some other examples:

Redundant	Oh really? As opposed to . . .	Concise
the unfortunate problem	. . . the fortunate problem?	the problem
advance warning	. . . a warning that comes afterwards?	warning
helpful cooperation	. . . annoying cooperation?	cooperation
a brilliant genius	. . . a stupid genius?	a genius

Your Turn

Here are some sentences that contain redundancies. Find the redundancies and say to yourself, "Oh really, as opposed to . . . ?" Then see if you can revise the sentences:

1. In today's contemporary society, we would be lost without the computer.

_____

2. The following sums up the basic essentials of our proposal.

_____

Here are our corrections:

1. **Improved:** Today, we would be lost without the computer.

   Or: In our society, we would be lost without the computer.

   Or: In contemporary society, we would be lost without the computer.

2. **Improved:** The following sums up the essentials of our proposal.

3. DON'T "GILD THE LILY"

Avoid needless qualification. Some words are absolute. They don't need to be qualified with words such as *very, somewhat, slightly,* or *extremely.* The most obvious example, of course, is *pregnant.* You're either pregnant or you're not—no one is *slightly pregnant.* Here are some other absolute words that shouldn't be qualified:

unique
Unique means "one of a kind." So don't say *rather unique* or *extremely unique,* and certainly not *totally unique.* As with pregnancy, either something is unique or it isn't.

absolute
Not surprisingly, this word is also absolute. Writing *completely absolute* is using unnecessary qualification.

wrong
Again, this is a strong, critical word. If you're going to use it, don't pull your punches by saying *very wrong,* or *totally wrong.*

Words that, while not absolute, are meant to be forceful can actually be weakened by qualification. For example, "You look stunning" is a stronger statement than "You look very stunning."

Your Turn

Read the following memo. Then get rid of the unnecessary qualifiers in each sentence and read it again. How does the revised memo sound? We think it packs a stronger punch.

A truly shocking matter has just come to our attention. Many employees are rather flagrantly ignoring the "No Smoking" signs in the company washrooms. This is a very serious breach of office etiquette. We would like this incredibly outrageous behavior to stop more or less immediately.

FYI, here's a revised, stronger memo. Notice how much stronger this second version sounds.

> A shocking matter has just come to our attention. Many employees are flagrantly ignoring the "No Smoking" signs in the company washrooms. This is a serious breach of office etiquette. We would like this outrageous behavior to stop immediately.

Finally, don't qualify words that are already qualified by definition. For example, the words *may* and *might* are self-qualifying. They carry with them the meaning "not necessarily," so don't write that you "may possibly" be late for lunch, or even worse, that you "may or may not" be late. The italicized words in the sentences below are unnecessary. Read each sentence, first with, then without the italicized words. See what we mean?

> We might *possibly* be held up by bad weather.

> We usually go to the beach on *most* sunny days.

It's difficult to generalize about writing. Sometimes an extra word or two does add a necessary emphasis or can clarify a writer's tone, even though the rules of writing would say not to use it. Look at the difference between these two sentences:

> I was exhausted.

> I was completely exhausted.

The second is different in meaning and intensity than the first. You might want to keep in the modifier *completely* to make the reader understand this was serious exhaustion, not your everyday tired-at-the-end-of-an-ordinary-workday exhaustion.

So if you find you absolutely must break the no-unnecessary-qualifiers rule, go ahead. Just be sure you are compelled to do it because of what you want to say, rather than because you feel the need to throw in an extra word or three. Wait a day after you have written the text. Look at it again. If the qualifiers that you edited out of your work scream to come back, you might consider leaving them in.

 11

4. AVOID PADDING

When you've said it all, you are through. Don't pad. Padding is writing words, phrases, or even whole sentences just to take up space. Writers who use padding are usually trying to make their piece of writing longer. This is what many college students do when they have ten pages worth of stuff to say, but the assignment is for a 20-page paper. They pad. Sorry, but this technique doesn't fool anyone. So, say what you have to say, and then stop writing. If you want to fill up the page, write bigger! (Just kidding.)

The sentences below are examples of padding. Following the sentences are either instructions or rewrites regarding the padding—simply get rid or it, or revise it to make it meaningful.

Padded: What I have just said supports my original point.

Advice: Get rid of the whole sentence.

Padded: Which idea of the author's points is more in line with what I believe? This is a very interesting question. First of all . . .

Rewrite: The author and I do agree on some points. First of all . . .

Padded: Now I'm going to take up a new point. What about the people who oppose recycling because it's too expensive? They are simply incorrect.

Rewrite: As for the people who oppose recycling because it's too expensive, they are simply incorrect.

Plug In

Remember, your mission as a writer is to be concise. Be tough, be ruthless, be efficient. Cut out any word that doesn't absolutely need to be there. Then go back and cut even more. In some cases you might want to combine two sentences into one.

Okay, now it's your turn to show how concise you can be. On the space provided, rewrite the sentences that need revision. Some may be fine just the way they are, so you can just leave them. One of the sentences needs a complete overhaul. Then check to see how we rewrote them and why.

1. Our work group reached a consensus of opinion.

   _____

2. We have decided that at the present time we need at least one printer for every four employees. The reason for that is because of the rather overwhelming volume of work generated by each employee.

   _____

3. Prior to the spring, we faced a rather typical problem.

   _____

4. Most employees are more or less ignorant of how to use their computers.

   _____

5. At this time, however, our situation is somewhat unique. Every single employee, without exception, has mastered his or her computer technology.

   _____

6. It is therefore extremely crucial that we upgrade our printer situation to make it more or less equal to the workload involved.

7. When Moby Dick escaped yet again, Captain Ahab's anger was plainly visible to the eye.

---

8. His crew members were totally terrified.

---

9. They knew his intense obsession would lead only to terrible disaster due to the fact of Ahab's complete and total control of everything and everybody on the ship.

---

10. What about the critics who say that Ahab's crew members could have prevented their captain's destructive course? I do not agree with them. Clearly, Ahab's crew had absolutely no choice.

Plug In Solutions

Here are our suggested revisions:

1. Our work group reached a consensus. (*Of opinion* is redundant.)

2. We have decided that we need at least one printer for every four employees because of the overwhelming volume of work generated by each employee. (*At the present time* and *The reason for that is* are wordy. *Rather* qualifies—and weakens—the forceful word, *overwhelming.*)

3. Before the spring, we faced a typical problem. (*Prior to* is wordy. *Rather* qualifies an absolute word.)

4. Most employees are more or less ignorant of how to use their computers. (This sentence is actually all right. You might take out *more or less*, but it does make the degree of employee ignorance more clear.)

5. Now, however, our situation is unique. Every employee has mastered his or her computer. (*At this time* is wordy. *Somewhat* qualifies an absolute word. *Single, without exception,* and *technology* are redundant.)

6. It is therefore crucial that we have enough printers to take care of our workload. (This sentence was just a mess. Did the writer mean *extremely crucial* as opposed to "just a little bit crucial"? What is a *printer situation*? Why would you want a situation to be *more or less equal* to the workload, rather than fully equal? And what did *involved* mean? In a case like this, it's best to just start over, rather than cutting or changing one or two words.)

7. When Moby Dick escaped yet again, Captain Ahab's anger was plainly visible. (Since Ahab's anger was presumably not visible to the ear, we cut *to the eye*. Whether to cut *plainly* is a tough call, but we liked the added emphasis. If you cut it anyway, give yourself extra points for conciseness.)

8. His crew members were terrified. (Since you can't be "partially" terrified, *totally* had to go.)

9. They knew his obsession would lead only to disaster due to Ahab's total control of everything on the ship. (All obsessions are by definition "intense," and all disasters are "terrible." *The fact of* is wordy; *complete and* is redundant; so is *and everybody*.)

10. Clearly, Ahab's crew had no choice. (The first two sentences were pure padding. *Absolutely* is redundant, though we might not quarrel if you left it in for extra emphasis.)

If your rewrites are close to ours, congratulations! You've mastered the ability to be concise. If you feel you need more practice, no problem. Take a break, then reread this chapter. Try this Plug In exercise once again and see how it goes.

CHAPTER TWO

Rule Two: Be Forceful

One of the scariest parts of writing is the sense of being exposed, or revealed, to your readers. What you write will let readers know something about you, so naturally, you may worry about what they'll think. After all, there is a blank, white page or a blank, bright computer screen, and what are you going to fill it with? You. Faced with that prospect, even an experienced writer has to fight the tendency to run screaming from the room, looking for an errand to run, a phone call to make, an oven to clean—but really, a place to hide.

> ⌁**POWER LINE**⌁
>
> One should never write down or up to people, but out of yourself.
>
> —Christopher Isherwood

DON'T DILUTE YOUR MESSAGE

If you don't actually run away and hide in the closet, you might want to hide behind lots of unnecessary words, as this poor writer has done:

> In my opinion, Amy Tan's books are just great. There are several reasons that her work is thrilling to readers. The characters are eminently believable and are presented with enormous facility. It can be seen that the author wants them to seem real. The stories are always interesting and fun to read. And the settings are so vivid that I, personally, felt like I was there myself. It seems to me that the author has learned to make her prose user-friendly. In my experience, this is the kind of an author whom everybody likes.

In our opinion, this kind of writing comes from insecurity. The writer may very well hold strong opinions about Amy Tan's books, but you would never know it from that paragraph. Instead of getting "out there" and expressing her opinions for all to see, the writer has hidden herself behind a screen of words and phrases.

Let us say our writer takes several deep breaths, repeats a few affirming thoughts, enrolls in assertiveness training, or, perhaps, reads this book. Then she produces a new, more forceful version of her work:

> Amy Tan's work is deeply moving and always entertaining. Her work draws in readers for several reasons. Tan clearly and skillfully presents her characters so that they seem like real people. She tells intriguing, mysterious stories. She draws vivid settings. She writes lovely prose. No wonder Tan is such a popular writer.

When we read the new paragraph, we not only get a sense of Amy Tan, we also get a sense of the writer, herself. By being forceful—by getting out there and expressing her ideas clearly and directly—our writer has revealed a part of herself to us, the readers. She has also written a fine paragraph.

POWER LINE

To be a good writer, you may not only have to write a great deal but you have to care. You do not have to have a complicated moral philosophy. But a writer always tries, I think, to be a part of the solution, to understand a little about life and to pass this on.

–Anne Lamott, *Bird By Bird*

If you would like your writing to be more forceful, you don't have to take an assertiveness training course (although you might want to take a few deep breaths or keep some affirming thoughts tacked up near your writing area). Instead, take a look at these suggestions and apply them to your work.

DON'T SAY "I" UNLESS YOU HAVE TO

Avoid needless self-reference. Reminding the reader that you are offering your own opinion is usually a way of discrediting yourself—as well as your opinion. The words, "In my opinion . . . " usually translate to "Only in my opinion . . . ," "In my humble opinion . . . ," or even worse, "In my opinion, which doesn't count for much." Readers will know the opinion you're stating is your own. Whose else would it be? So just leave references to yourself, such as *my, mine, I,* and *me* out of it, and say what you have to say.

Your Turn

Read the following sentences aloud, using the tone of voice they seem to invite. Then read them without the italicized self-references. How does the tone change?

> *My guess is that* most people take the First Amendment for granted. *Although I'm not an expert, I tend to think that* all of us fall into this trap from time to time. *I must emphasize,* however, *that in my opinion,* failing to value free speech can be even more dangerous than actively supporting censorship.

Here are some other examples of self-reference that insecure writers use to "hedge their bets," or deliberately make their opinions sound less forceful:

I feel	In my experience
I think	In my personal opinion
I believe	As far as I am concerned
It is my opinion/belief/feeling that . . .	

However, in some cases, you might want to use the I-word. Perhaps the subject of your writing is yourself—how you learned to ski, why you want to go to business school, why you love chocolate, how you felt when your microwave oven exploded—then feel free to say *I,* as in this example:

> I am a chocolate lover and proud of it. I have always found that chocolate lovers are reliable, upstanding people, while those who don't like chocolate seem to me to be shifty, untrustworthy folks.

Otherwise, avoid the I-word if you can. If you are writing an academic paper or exam, or if you're drafting a business proposal, you had better avoid using self-references altogether.

USE THE ACTIVE VOICE

Verbs come in two voices, *active* and *passive*. Generally, active sounds more forceful. For example:

> **Active:** Congress soon *passed* the new speed limit for roller-bladers.

> **Passive:** The new speed limit for in-line skaters *was soon passed* by Congress.

Get the difference? In the active version, someone or something *takes action*—Congress passes a new speed limit. In the passive version, something *is acted upon*—the new speed limit was passed by Congress. In general, avoid the passive voice, as active voice makes your writing sound more forceful.

However, rules always have exceptions, and here are a couple.

⌁⌁ **POWER LINE** ⌁⌁

The habitual use of the active voice . . . makes for forcible writing. This is true not only in narrative concerned principally with action but in writing of any kind. Many a tame sentence of description or exposition can be made lively and emphatic by substituting a transitive in the active voice for some such perfunctory expression as *there is* or *could be heard*.

—Strunk and White, *Elements of Style*

- What if you don't know who's taking the action, only the result? Then you're stuck with the passive voice:

Last year's champion team was defeated. (By whom, we have no idea.)

- Sometimes (rarely), the passive voice actually supports your meaning, because you really want to emphasize the way the subject has been acted upon, and you're not particularly interested in who did the acting. For example:

When they were children, Deirdre was allowed to stay up late, but Cory wasn't.

This sentence is about Deirdre and Cory—not about their parents who allowed or didn't allow. The active voice would weaken the sentence, make it long and awkward, and shift the importance away from Deirdre and Cory:

> When Deirdre and Cory were children, their parents allowed Deirdre to stay up late, but not Cory.

Active or Passive Voice? The general rule for effective writing is, "Use the active voice—almost always."

COME ON STRONG!

Avoid weak constructions. Starting a sentence with *it* or *there* usually makes a sentence weaker. Remember, it's better to just come out and say what you have to say, without hiding behind extra, unnecessary words. Here are some examples.

> **Weak:** It would be useless to send the text without a diagram.
> **Forceful:** Sending the text without a diagram would be useless.

> **Weak:** There is general agreement that fruit doesn't belong on pizza.
> **Forceful:** Most people agree that fruit doesn't belong on pizza.

> **Weak:** It seems that the green carpeting clashes with the purple drapes.
> **Forceful:** The green carpeting clashes with the purple drapes.

> **Weak:** There is milk in the refrigerator that has gone bad.
> **Forceful:** The milk in the refrigerator has gone bad.

Of course, sometimes *it* and *there* refer to specific things or places and have a perfectly legitimate place at the beginning of sentence:

> *There* was my other sock—well part of it, anyway. *It* hung limply from the puppy's mouth.

There may be times when it's perfectly okay to use these "weak" constructions. It is not always necessary to avoid them. For example, look at the two sentences you just read. Maybe the following two sentences sound stronger:

> So-called weak constructions are sometimes perfectly acceptable. Avoiding them is not always necessary.

AVOID VAGUE LANGUAGE

Be specific. The more specific your writing, the more quickly and easily your readers will grasp your point. Let us go back to our friend, the writer. Here is an excerpt from her vague first draft, followed by her more forceful revision:

> **Weak and Vague:** Amy Tan's books are just great. . . . The stories are always interesting and fun to read.

> **Strong and Specific:** Amy Tan's work is deeply moving and always entertaining. . . . She tells intriguing, mysterious stories.

The first example makes clear that the writer likes Amy Tan, but we really don't learn much more. The second example tells why the writer likes Tan. It might even convince us to read some of her books. Here is the same writer describing a favorite movie.

> **Weak and Vague:** *Casablanca* is a great movie. It was interesting and fun to watch.

> **Strong and Specific:** *Casablanca* is one of the most romantic movies I have ever seen. There is an electricity between Humphrey Bogart and Lauren Bacall. The sharp, quick dialogue kept me on the edge of my seat. I really cared what happened to the characters. At the end of the movie I had become so caught up in the situation of Bogart and Bacall that I cried.

Caution: Vague Words! Each of the following words holds up a sign saying "Caution: Vague Word." When you read over your writing and find any of these, ask yourself which word would be more specific. Then use it! Here is our vague-word "hit list":

good	bad	pretty	excellent	nice
boring	terrible	great	mean	
interesting				

THE 5 W'S AND H

How do you find more specific words to use in your writing? Keep asking yourself questions. (After all, better you than your reader!) Newspaper reporters use a set of six questions known as The 5 W's and H: Who? What? Where? When? Why? and How?

Apply these questions to any of the vague words we've identified earlier. For example:

Vague: Gina is an excellent employee.

Okay, good for Gina, but what exactly does she do? How does she show how excellent she is? Why does she deserve our praise? Try changing the word *excellent* to a more specific word that tells in what ways Gina is so great: *loyal, enthusiastic, hard-working, highly skilled.* You may find that you need to use several specific words to replace one vague one.

Specific: Gina is a loyal, enthusiastic, hard-working, and highly skilled employee.

Yes, we know, we just broke that rule about never using several words when one will do. But in this case, one won't do. And anyway, you've probably gotten the idea by now that writing rules always have exceptions. In fact, knowing when to follow a rule and when to make an exception is one of the keys to powerful writing. As you practice and pay attention to your writing, you'll get the knack.

AVOID CLICHÉS

A cliché is a word or phrase that's been used so many times and for so long, that no one pays attention to its real meaning any more. Here are some examples:

You look pretty as a picture.

It's like looking for a needle in a haystack.

It was raining cats and dogs.

Each of these expressions, when it was first used about eight million years ago, was original and fresh, and let the reader know what the writer meant. Now, such expressions have been used so much that they've lost their original meanings. When you read, for example, "It was raining cats and dogs," you know the writer meant, "It was raining hard," but you don't actually visualize cats and dogs falling from the sky, as you probably would if you'd never heard the expression before. If you want to emphasize how hard it was raining, you'll have to do it some other way that's more original:

It was raining so hard, I needed windshield wipers for my glasses.

It was raining so hard, I felt like I was in the shower with my clothes on.

It might even be enough to simply say, "It was raining hard." The important thing to remember is that clichés are boring, and no one pays attention to them. The more clichés you use in your writing, the more you'll bore your readers, and the less attention readers will pay to what you have to say. They'll say to themselves, "I have heard all this before"—and they'll be right.

POWER LINE

Choose your words with unusual care. If a phrase comes to you easily, look at it with deep suspicion—it's probably one of the innumerable clichés that have woven their way so tightly into the fabric of travel writing that it takes a special effort not to use them . . . .

–William Zinsser, *On Writing Well*

AVOID JARGON

Jargon used to mean the specialized vocabulary of a profession, such as *tibia* and *fibula* for doctors, or *Statue of Liberty play* for football coaches. Now jargon has taken on a second meaning: the overly inflated, meaningless, or semi-meaningless words that have somehow become the language of business and politics. Here are some examples:

This decision will positively *impact* our productivity.

We want our products to be as *user-friendly* as possible.

Please *finalize* these plans by next week.

The *bottom line* is that we need to increase our profits.

The problem with jargon is similar to the problem with clichés: They're both boring. Use enough jargon, and pretty soon your readers' eyes will glaze over, and it will all start to sound like, "blah, blah, blah, blah, blah." In addition, jargon can make your writing impossible to understand. In fact, it's often used for just this purpose. For example, read the sentences below.

Jargon Filled: We intend to designate new parameters for optimal employee participation in the company, and to target year-end norms for employee output. This will enable us to optimize the size of our workforce and facilitate downsizing by year end.

Jargon Free: We will require each employee to do more work, so that we can lay off more people.

Okay, so the original jargon-laden memo had a little bit more detail than that. But think it through. What does it actually mean? The writer of the memo was not only a bad writer, but also a coward, afraid to come out and say what had to be said, even if it was unpleasant. The writer was definitely breaking the "Be forceful" rule, hiding behind words instead of using them to communicate meaning. Here's how the memo could have been worded without the jargon, but with a little more tact:

Jargon Free, With Tact: We plan to assign new work requirements to each employee, so that by the end of the year, everyone will be working up to capacity. At that time, we will be able to reduce the number of jobs, which will greatly benefit our company.

Detecting Jargon. How can you tell when a word is jargon? Here are some clues:

- Nouns used as verbs (*impact, target, benefit*)
- Hyphenated words (*user-friendly, goal-oriented*)
- Neologisms, or newly created words (*interface, downsize, bottom line, time frame*)

Up to now, we have cautioned you to use your own judgment, advising you break rules when you feel you absolutely must. With jargon, we would like to be a bit more strict: Don't use it! Certainly don't use it if you're writing a college entrance exam or academic paper, if you are writing for any type of publication (such as a letter to the editor), or for any general audience (such as a letter to a store manager). If you are writing for work—"a job situation," we almost said, being not entirely jargon free ourselves—you might consider jargon if you believe that this is the kind of language to which your readers will best respond. However, if you are the one person in your office who does not use jargon, you might discover that yours are the only memos in your office that do get read.

Plug In

Now it's your turn to root out weak language of all types, creating forceful sentences that confront the reader with clear, well thought out ideas. Rewrite each sentence.

Where necessary, eliminate self-reference, the passive voice, weak openings, vague language, complicated or abstract language, clichés, and jargon. However, where those devices are effective, leave them alone. You be the judge! Then read on to find out what we decided. (P.S. If you find vague language anywhere, make up your own specific details to replace it.)

1. With reference to the "Star-Spangled Banner," I, like many people, have always considered it almost impossible to sing well.

2. It is obvious that this song should only be sung by experts.

_____

3. There are many interesting characters in this book.

_____

4. By the end of the book I felt the characters had become old friends.

_____

5. The optimal choice would be to implement employee training programs at the earliest available point in time.

_____

6. Such programs would be intended to maximize employee productivity while minimizing company expenditures.

_____

7. I have wanted to be a scientist since I first laid eyes on a microscope, but it was only last year that I realized why I want to be a scientist.

_____

8. The week my first experiment was conducted, I was required to work like a dog, but the results were well worth it.

_____

Plug In Solutions

Here are our suggested revisions for the Plug In sentences:

1. Many people find the "Star-Spangled Banner" almost impossible to sing well. (weak beginning; unnecessary self-reference)
2. Clearly, only experts should sing this song. (weak beginning; passive voice)
3. Many characters in the book are intriguing. (weak beginning; vague)
4. By the end of the book, the characters have the weird familiarity of old, half-remembered yearbook pictures. (unnecessary self-reference; cliché)
5. The company should begin employee training programs as soon as possible. (jargon)
6. These programs will make employees more productive while saving the company money. (passive voice; jargon)
7. I have wanted to be a scientist since I saw my first microscope, but I never realized why I wanted to be scientist until last year. (cliché; weak language)
8. The week I conducted my first experiment, I worked harder than I'd ever worked in my life—but the results were well worth it. (passive voice; cliché)

Your rewrites don't have to match ours word for word, but if you came close to ours, congratulations. If not, carefully compare your work with ours. Which version do you prefer? If you like our choices better, see if you can tell why we made them. Then apply that kind of powerful thinking to your own writing and revision.

CHAPTER THREE

Rule Three: Be Correct

Be correct in your writing, or, "follow the rules of writing." We really struggled over whether to include this rule. After all, the fear of not being correct is what keeps many people from writing at all. Or, if they're absolutely forced to write, they

∿∿ POWER LINE ∿∿

It is wise not to violate the rules until you know how to use them.

–T.S. Eliot

feel insecure and anxious. Like soldiers crossing a minefield, they want to get in and get out as quickly as possible. Finally, nobody likes being nagged.

On the other hand, certain rules of writing actually do make your writing clearer and easier to follow. Honestly, they are there to help you reach your readers, so that your writing flows more smoothly and rhythmically and your thoughts emerge more clearly. If you don't follow these rules, your readers may not even realize it. They'll just sense, somehow, that your sentences don't quite work.

The good news is that these rules are really quite simple. Once you know about them, it is much easier to fix a sentence that seems to have gone mysteriously awry. Think of them as a repair checklist, like that troubleshooting page you get when you buy a new TV—you know, the one that lists "Problems" in one column, "Probable Cause" in another, and "What to Do" in a third. So here goes. We'll try to make the rules of writing as painless as possible.

MAKE SURE SUBJECTS AND VERBS AGREE

Repeat after us: "Singular subjects go with singular verbs, and plural subjects go with plural verbs." In other words, "The three *witches dance* around the steaming cauldron," (plural subject, plural verb) but then, "One *witch dances* towards Macbeth with a dreadful secret" (singular subject, singular verb).

So far, so good, and you probably knew about agreement already. However, it can get tricky, as in the following circumstances:

> ◦✳◦ **POWER LINE** ◦✳◦
>
> Words that intervene between subject and verb do not affect the number of the verb.
>
> –Strunk and White, *Elements of Style*

- When the subject and verb are separated by a number of words:

The *witch*, glancing gleefully at her sisters, *smiles* at the frightened Macbeth. (singular subject, singular noun)

- When the subject is a collective noun:

A *coven* of witches *was* meeting that night. ("Coven" is singular, even though it is made up of more than one person. Same goes for a *flock* of birds, a *herd* of cows, a *pride* of lions, and so on.)

- When the subject consists of more than one noun:

Macbeth, who wanted to be King, *and his wife*, who wanted even more to be Queen, *were* thrilled by the witches' prophecy. (The subject, "Macbeth and his wife," is plural and takes a plural verb.)

- When two nouns are linked by *either . . . or*:

Either Macbeth or Lady Macbeth has to murder the king. ("Either . . . or" means "one or the other, but not both." Therefore it takes a singular verb. This last example is the trickiest, because the subject *looks* plural, but isn't.)

Here are a few more examples of singular subjects that seem to be plural:

- *Each* of the club members *has* to pay dues.
- Every club *member has* to pay dues.
- The whole *audience was* cheering.
- *Macbeth*, along with his wife, *is* drawn deeper and deeper into a web of murder and deceit.

About that last example: If the main part of the subject were plural, the verb would be plural. For example: The *soldiers*, along with their general, *are* in a dangerous situation. However, the sentence would read better if the main part of the subject were closer to the verb, as in:

- Along with their general, the *soldiers* are in a dangerous situation.
- Along with his wife, *Macbeth* is drawn deeper and deeper . . . .

Just to make life more interesting, you need to know about some tricky little words called *indefinite pronouns*. Sometimes it's hard to tell if they're singular or plural. For example:

Singular: *Everybody* at the concert *was* shouting.

Plural: *Some* of the audience *were* running for the door, while *others were* heading for the stage.

Indefinite Pronouns that Are Always Singular. Here's the list:

anybody	everybody	somebody	either one	another
anyone	everyone	someone	neither	each
anything	everything	something	no one	

Indefinite Pronouns that Are Always Plural. Here's the list:

both	few	many	several	others

Indefinite Pronouns that Are Sometimes Singular and Sometimes Plural.
Now, to make the rules of writing even more interesting, here are the indefinite
pronouns that can be singular or plural, depending on how they are used:

all	any	more	most
some	one-half	none	

If one of the above pronouns refers to a singular noun, the pronoun is singular.
If the pronoun refers to a plural noun, it's plural.

> **Singular:** *Most* of the *cheesecake* has been eaten. *None* of the
> *cheesecake* has been eaten.

> **Plural:** *Most* of the *cheesecakes* have been sold. *None* of the
> *cheesecakes* have been sold.

USE *YOU* APPROPRIATELY

In this book we have taken a friendly, informal tone and addressed you, our
audience, as *you*. In more technical terms, we have been using the *second person*.

When It's Okay to Use *You*. Follow these rules, and you won't misuse *you*:

- The second person is appropriate for how-to writing, in which you
  tell your readers how to do something—how to build a birdhouse or
  make a blueberry pie.

- Using *you* is also appropriate—indeed, required—for most letters: If
  you don't give me a full refund for that piece of junk you just sold
  me, you can expect some pretty serious consequences, Mr. Jones.

- On the job, *you* is generally appropriate for memos and speeches.

When It's Not Okay to Use *You*. Follow these rules about when you shouldn't
use *you*:

- Refrain from using the second person in the more formal writing
  you do for school or on the job.

- *You* is not appropriate in most college entrance essays, exams, and
  term papers.

- Don't use the second person for proposals or progress reports. For example, instead of writing "As *you* can see, the following suggestions will improve employee morale," write, "Clearly, the following suggestions will improve employee morale," or just, "The following suggestions will improve employee morale." No *you*.

Sometimes the word *you* is used to mean "everyone," as in the sentence "*You* can never be too careful." If you are writing a formal letter or essay, you'll have to switch from the second person to the *third person*. Use the word *one* instead: "*One* can never be too careful." That sounds fine, but using the word *one* over and over again doesn't sound fine at all. You can avoid the problem altogether by using a plural subject. For example:

Too Informal: You never know how hard you've been working until you take a vacation.

Formal and Awkward: One never knows how hard one has been working until one takes a vacation.

Better, Using the Plural: Most people don't know how hard they've been working until they take a vacation.

USE PRONOUNS CORRECTLY

Since we're on the subject of pronouns, this seems like a good time to discuss them further. A *pronoun* is a word that replaces a noun in a sentence. Every time you use a pronoun—*he, him, his, she, her, it, its, they, their, that,* or *which*—you are always referring to an *antecedent*—a particular person, place, thing, or idea that, presumably, you have already mentioned. Your readers must always know exactly to what your pronoun is referring. Otherwise, they'll get confused. Here are some examples:

Confusing: The mother was disturbed about her daughter because she didn't agree with her values.

Repetitious: The mother was disturbed because her daughter didn't agree with her mother's values.

Clear: The mother was disturbed because she didn't agree with her daughter's values.

The secret to a clear use of pronouns is to look at every pronoun you've used in a sentence, and ask yourself the question, "who?" or "what?" In the confusing sentence above, it's hard to answer the question, "who?" when you come to the pronoun she. Who is *she*—the mother or the daughter? The repetitious sentence is clear because the writer used a noun (*daughter*) instead of a pronoun (*she*). Yet this sentence is clumsy and wordy. In the final sentence, you can easily answer the question "who is *she*?" The pronoun she in this sentence clearly refers to the mother. And in addition to being clear, the sentence is also concise.

Sometimes *it, this, that,* or *which* are used to refer to an entire phrase or an idea. Using pronouns in this way can be dangerous. It's usually better to use a noun. For example:

Unclear:	The lead guitarist swayed back and forth, gyrated his hips, and threw back his head. This made the audience go wild. (What exactly got the audience so worked up— all three actions together or just the last?)
Clear:	The lead guitarist swayed back and forth, gyrated his hips, and threw back his head. These antics made the audience go wild.
Also Clear:	The lead guitarist swayed back and forth, gyrated his hips, and threw back his head. This final gesture made the audience go wild.

You are also entering a danger zone when you use a pronoun to refer to an antecedent that you haven't actually named—in other words, a nonexistent antecedent. For example:

Unclear:	As the guitarist played, it got louder and louder. (What got louder and louder? We probably would have figured out what you meant sooner or later, but your writing will read more smoothly if you make your antecedents clear.)
Clear:	As the guitarist played, the music got louder and louder.

THE *HE-SHE* CONTROVERSY

Once upon a time, in the bad old days, whenever a singular indefinite pronoun (*everyone, each,* etcetera) was used, writers always assumed that it referred to *he,* unless they were talking about all-female groups, like mothers or nuns. The rule was: When in doubt, use *he.* We don't use that rule anymore.

> **Old Usage:** When the fire drill began, *everyone* in the classroom reached for *his* books and headed for the hall. (Unless you were talking about an all-boys school, the women in the classroom were being left to burn. So new usages were born.)

> **New (But Awkward):** When the fire drill began, *everyone* in the classroom reached for *his* or *her* books and headed for the hall. (The best way to avoid having to say *he* or *she* or *his* or *her* is to make the whole sentence plural.)

> **Less Awkward:** When the fire drill began, *all the students* in the classroom reached for *their* books and headed for the hall.

Some people even feel free to write: "*Everyone* reached for *their* books . . . ." If using a plural verb with a singular subject were acceptable, this would be a great way to avoid the whole problem. But it is *not* acceptable. Some people will penalize you for it, particularly in an academic setting or on an entrance exam. The safer route is to find ways to use either *he or she* or *they.* Or you might do as we have sometimes done and alternate, using *he* sometimes and *she* sometimes. If you take that route, just be sure that you give both genders equal time, and that you don't refer to all the doctors as *he,* and all the nurses as *she.* No stereotyping.

〜〜 POWER LINE 〜〜

The best solutions simply eliminate the male pronouns and connotations by altering some component of the sentence. 'We' is a useful substitute for 'he'; 'the' can often replace 'his'; general nouns can replace specific nouns: (A) 'First he notices what's happening to his kids and he blames it on his neighborhood.' (B) 'First we notice what's happening to our kids and we blame it on the neighborhood.' (A) 'Doctors often neglect their wives and children.' (B) 'Doctors often neglect their families.' Countless sins can be erased by such small changes.

–William Zinsser, *On Writing Well*

USE PARALLEL CONSTRUCTION EFFECTIVELY

"I came, I saw, I conquered." That Julius Caesar sure knew how to use parallel construction! He would have been equally correct, although probably less memorable, if he'd said, "I came, saw, and conquered." But he would have been in trouble if he'd said, "I came, saw, and I conquered." The idea is to be consistent. If Caesar decided to leave out the "I" before "saw" and "conquered," fine. But leaving out the "I" for "saw," and putting it back in for "conquered"— not fine. It doesn't even sound right. Here's another example:

> **Not Parallel:** Labrador retrievers are gentle, intelligent, and make good pets.
>
> "Gentle" and "intelligent" are adjectives, or describing words; "make" is a verb, or action word.
>
> **Parallel:** Labrador retrievers are gentle, intelligent, and easily trained.
>
> "Easily trained" is an adjective phrase, or describing phrase.

Your Turn

Since understanding parallel construction isn't easy, here is a chance for you to try focusing on this difference. Decide whether each sentence is parallel or not parallel (underline your pick):

1. A new athletic program is both worthwhile and a necessity. (parallel, not parallel)
2. One sees interesting wildlife on the ground, in the trees, and flying. (parallel, not parallel)
3. A new athletic program is both worthwhile and necessary. (parallel, not parallel)
4. One sees interesting wildlife on the ground, in the trees, and in the air. (parallel, not parallel)
5. One sees interesting wildlife crawling, running, climbing, and flying. (parallel, not parallel)
6. Our office manager has investigated the situation, compared various prices, and has made her choice. (parallel, not parallel)

7. Our office manager has investigated the situation, compared various prices, and made her choice. (parallel, not parallel)

8. Winning is not as important as how you play the game. (parallel, not parallel)

9. Our office manager has investigated the situation, has compared various prices, and has made her choice. (parallel, not parallel)

10. Winning is not as important as playing well. (parallel, not parallel)

How did you do? Check out these answers and explanations:

1. Not parallel: "Worthwhile" is an adjective; "necessity" is a noun.

2. Not parallel: "On the ground" and "in the trees" are prepositional phrases. "Flying" is an adjective.

3. Parallel: Both "worthwhile" and "necessary" are adjectives.

4. Parallel: "On the ground," "in the trees," and "in the air" are all prepositional phrases.

5. Parallel: "Crawling," "running," "climbing," and "flying" are all adjectives.

6. Not Parallel: "Has" is left out for "compared various prices," but put back in for "made her choice."

7. Parallel: No "has" for "compared various prices" or "made her choice."

8. Not Parallel: "Winning" and "how to" are not the same part of speech.

9. Parallel: "Has" is used uniformly throughout the sentence.

10. Parallel: "Winning" and "playing" are the same parts of speech.

Just when you think you've gotten it figured out, here's an especially tricky example. What if some items in a sentence take *a*, and some take *an*?

Not Parallel: Our office now has a water cooler, air-conditioner, and coffee-maker.

Parallel: Our office now has a water cooler, an air-conditioner, and a coffee-maker.

And what if some items are singular and some are plural?

> **Not Parallel:** We also have a new VCR, slide projector, tape player, and numerous videotapes.

> **Parallel:** We also have a new VCR, a slide projector, a tape player, and numerous videotapes.

PUT MODIFIERS IN THE RIGHT PLACE

"Modifier" is a fancy word that just means "a word or phrase that tells more about another word in a sentence." For example, in the sentence, "Mr. Lopez spoke to us during lunch," "during lunch" is a modifier. It tells when Mr. Lopez spoke. So far, so good, but just put a modifier in the wrong place, and you find that you're getting laughs when you meant to be serious.

> **Misplaced Modifier:** Mr. Lopez told us about his trip to Puerto Rico during his lunch hour. (Unless Mr. Lopez's lunch hour is very long indeed, the author has probably made a mistake.)

> **Correct:** During his lunch hour, Mr. Lopez told us about his trip to Puerto Rico.

> **Dangling Modifier:** Having worked in publishing for ten years, Mr. Lopez's daughter has a huge collection of books. (What a busy girl! We wonder what Mr. Lopez did for the ten years that his daughter was working.)

> **Correct:** Having worked in publishing for ten years, Mr. Lopez has provided his daughter with a huge collection of books.

> **Misplaced Modifier:** The banana was thrown by a student in a wastebasket. (This is an old favorite! What were they doing in there, anyway?)

> **Correct:** The banana was thrown in a wastebasket by a student.

> **Also correct:** A student threw the banana in a wastebasket.

As a rule, keep your modifiers as close as possible to the words they modify. As you read over your writing, make sure there's no question about which words modify what. Even the best of us misplace the occasional modifier or leave one dangling. Just try to catch these little errors when you look back over your writing.

38 **KAPLAN**

Plug In

Once again, it's your turn to bring correctness and clarity to the misshapen sentences below. Remember: Powerful writing comes from knowing what you want to say, and then saying it clearly. Using words correctly can help make your writing both clear and direct. Keep the following principles in mind:

- Make sure subjects and verbs agree.
- Use *you* correctly.
- Use pronouns correctly.
- Know how to use *he, she,* and *they*.
- Use parallel construction effectively.
- Put modifiers in the right place.

In the space provided, revise the following sentences. Then check to see how we rewrote them and why.

1. He, along with the other committee members, believe that this policy is ineffective.

   _____

2. One might even say that the policy is unfair, but you would be going too far.

   _____

3. If employees want to learn more about this policy, you can read the complete report on file in Ms. Jenkins's office.

   _____

4. Mr. Lee told Mr. Abrams that he was getting a raise.

   _____

5. More than one employee is regularly oversleeping in this office!

_____

6. Lateness is bad enough, but the people who leave early have a terrible effect on company morale.

_____

7. Everyone must be responsible for the way their behavior affects their co-workers.

_____

8. The most important qualities in an assistant are punctuality, accuracy, and he must be organized.

_____

9. Every employee will receive an envelope containing his bonus check.

_____

10. When searching for a job, a good résumé is helpful.

_____

Plug In Solutions

Here are our suggested revisions:

1. Along with the other committee members, he believes that this policy is ineffective. (subject-verb agreement)
2. Some people might even say that the policy is unfair, but they would be going too far. (using "you" correctly)

3. If employees want to learn more about this policy, they can read the complete report on file in Ms. Jenkins's office. (using—or not using—"you" correctly)

4. Mr. Lee told Mr. Abrams that Abrams was getting a raise. Another alternative: Mr. Lee told Mr. Abrams that Lee was getting a raise. (using pronouns correctly)

5. More than one employee in this office is regularly oversleeping! (misplaced modifier)

6. Arriving late is bad enough, but leaving early has a terrible effect on company morale. (parallel construction)

7. All employees must be responsible for the way their behavior affects their co-workers. (using "his," "hers," and "their" correctly)

8. The most important qualities in an assistant are punctuality, accuracy, and organization. An alternative: A good assistant must be punctual, accurate, and well-organized. (parallel construction)

9. All employees will receive envelopes containing their bonus checks. Another alternative: Every employee will receive an envelope containing his or her bonus check. (using "their" or "his or her" correctly)

10. Job seekers will find that a good résumé is helpful. Another alternative: When searching for a job, one will find that a good résumé is helpful. (misplaced modifier)

Sometimes you can correct your own writing by just changing a word or two; other times you have to rewrite a whole sentence from scratch. But always try to "be correct" and follow the rules to make your writing more powerful!

CHAPTER FOUR

Rule Four: Be Polished

You've learned to be concise, forceful, and correct. Now it's time to polish your writing and attend to details. The details we'll discuss may seem tiny, but they add up. They can help

POWER LINE

Be Obscure Clearly.

—E. B. White

determine whether people will take your writing seriously or dismiss it as sloppy. In short, they can increase your writing power.

USE CASUAL SPEECH APPROPRIATELY

Slang is informal conversational speech. Such words and phrases as "weird," "into music," and "wicked smart" are *colloquialisms*.

Some writers have made a specialty of using slang and colloquialisms, either in fiction writing or in humorous, personal essays. If you admire the work of, say, Alice Walker or Dave Barry, you'll notice their masterful use of common speech. And if you're doing similar work, we say, more power to you.

But if you are writing a college entrance essay or exam, an academic paper, a business memo, or another kind of formal writing, we suggest you stay away from informal, colloquial speech, at least until you determine whether such speech is acceptable to the people who will be reading and judging it. After all, in some offices, you are allowed to wear blue jeans, and some professors actually welcome informal language. Usually, though, professors and employers require formal English and formal dress. Choose your words accordingly.

DON'T FRAGMENT YOUR MESSAGE

A *sentence fragment* is an incomplete sentence. It is either missing a subject or a predicate, or it begins with a subordinating conjunction. Examples of such conjunctions are: *because, since, before,* and *unless.* There are many others. Here are some sentence fragments in action, with our suggested fixes, of course.

> **Missing a Predicate:** *The horrors of slavery.* That's what Toni Morrison's Pulitzer Prize–winning novel, *Beloved,* is all about.

> **Complete Sentence:** The horrors of slavery are a central concern in Toni Morrison's Pulitzer Prize–winning novel, *Beloved.*

> **Begins with a Subordinating Conjunction:** Why does Morrison's book include so many harrowing scenes? *Because she wants readers to realize the true costs of the slave system.*

> **Complete Sentence:** Morrison's book includes many harrowing scenes, so that readers will realize the true costs of the slave system.

We are the last to counsel against sentence fragments, having used about a dozen in this book alone. But then, this book has a more or less *informal* style. If we were writing an academic paper, a journalistic article, or a business letter, we would avoid sentence fragments. And we advise you to do the same.

In case you were wondering, a sentence that begins with *and, but, or,* or *so* is not technically considered a fragment. However, many people consider it less than formal writing, so use that construction in moderation, if at all.

BOYCOTT RUN-ON SENTENCES

While we may be ambivalent about fragments, we're quite decided about *run-on sentences:* Do not use them. As the name suggests, this type of sentence just goes on and on and on. Some run-ons may be grammatically correct, but they are simply too long. They consist of more than two sentences linked by conjunctions like *and, but,* or *or.* They may also include clauses that begin with *which, that,* or subordinating conjunctions. Here is an example and correction:

Run-on: Morrison drew on slave narratives for her novel, which was an excellent strategy, because it lends a ring of authenticity to her book, which distinguishes it from many other books written about slavery that simply aren't as powerful.

Rewrite: Morrison drew on slave narratives for her novel. This excellent strategy lends a ring of authenticity to her book, distinguishing it from other, less powerful stories of slavery.

Another type of run-on simply sticks two sentences together, without any punctuation or linking word:

Run-on: Morrison is one of my favorite writers her work is always challenging.

Rewrite: Morrison is one of my favorite writers. Her work is always challenging.

Alternative: Morrison is one of my favorite writers, because her work is always challenging.

Avoid Common Run-On Sentences. Be careful with adverbs like *however, nevertheless, furthermore, likewise,* and *therefore.* They should either begin a whole sentence of their own, or they should be preceded by a semicolon. If you use them to stick two sentences together (and you don't add a semicolon), you're creating a monster run-on.

Run-on: Morrison's characters experience terrible tragedy nevertheless their hope for the future finally prevails.

Rewrite: Morrison's characters experience terrible tragedy. Nevertheless, their hope for the future finally prevails.

Alternative: Morrison's characters experience terrible tragedy; nevertheless, their hope for the future finally prevails.

USE COMMAS CORRECTLY

Here are the six basic rules for using commas. Follow them, and your writing will show careful attention to some important details.

1. Use commas to separate three or more items in a series.

   Wrong: The experiment required us to record the weight color and density of the unknown substance.

   Correct: The experiment required us to record the weight, color, and density of the unknown substance.

2. Don't put a comma before the first item or after the last item in a series.

   Wrong: We were given, scales, a spectroscope, and a microscope. (comma before first item)

   Correct: We were given scales, a spectroscope, and a microscope.

   Wrong: Louis Pasteur, Marie Curie, and Charles Drew, all had similar concerns. (comma after last item)

   Correct: Louis Pasteur, Marie Curie, and Charles Drew all had similar concerns.

3. Use commas to separate two or more adjectives before a noun. But don't put a comma between the last adjective and the noun.

   Wrong: The substance was a thick, ochre, liquid. (comma between last adjective and noun)

   Correct: The substance was a thick, ochre liquid.

4. Use commas to set apart a clause that isn't necessary, or essential, to the sentence's main idea. This rule wins the prize for driving the most people crazy! We think that we should win the prize for having the best, easiest way to explain it.

KAPLAN

How to Find Nonessential Clauses. Here goes: The best way to identify a *nonessential clause* is to ask yourself if you could put the clause in parentheses. Do not actually use parentheses, but see if you could. If the answer is yes, the clause isn't essential, or necessary to the basic meaning of the sentence. If you took it out entirely, it wouldn't change the meaning. Therefore, it gets commas—one at the beginning and one at the end. For example:

Human beings, who do not have gills, cannot breathe under water.

If you put "who do not have gills" in parentheses, or even took it out, you wouldn't change the meaning of the sentence. But if you left out the commas and wrote, "Human beings who do not have gills cannot breathe under water," you'd be implying that some human beings do have gills.

If the answer is no, and the clause is basic to the meaning of the sentence, the clause is essential. Therefore it does not get any commas. Here's a sentence with an essential clause:

Most human beings who have blonde hair come from Nordic countries.

You would never put "who have blonde hair" in parentheses. If you did, or if you took it out, your sentence would imply that most human beings come from Nordic countries.

5.   Commas set off introductory words. This one is quick and easy:

> **Wrong:** However we are not always aware of what to do about this. (The word "however" should have a comma after it. It is an introductory word.)

> **Correct:** Fortunately, human beings have invented means of controlling their environment. Unfortunately, they have destroyed much of their environment while controlling it.

6.   Use a comma before *and, or, for, but,* or *yet* when you join two whole sentences together.

> **Wrong:** We were afraid the experiment would fail yet we continued.

> **Correct:** We were afraid the experiment would fail, yet we continued.

Wrong: My lab partner and I began by working separately but eventually we pooled our results.

Correct: My lab partner and I began by working separately, but eventually we pooled our results.

USE SEMICOLONS CORRECTLY

There are three rules for semicolons. Follow these little details, and they'll add to the generally powerful impression your writing will convey to readers.

1. Use semicolons in place of words such as *and*, *or*, or *but* to join two closely related sentences.

> ○W∿○ **POWER LINE** ○W∿○
>
> The semicolon should be used sparingly by writers of nonfiction today. Yet I notice that it turns up often in excerpts I've quoted in this book, and I've used it here myself more than I ordinarily do, mainly for the classic purpose of weighing two sides of the same problem.
>
> —William Zinsser, *On Writing Well*

Before: Science is my favorite subject and that's why I want to attend a school with a good science department.

After: Science is my favorite subject; that's why I want to attend a school with a good science department.

2. Use semicolons before words like *therefore*, *nevertheless*, and *moreover*.

Before: All through high school science was my favorite subject nevertheless, I also found time to try out for every school play.

After: All through high school, science was my favorite subject; nevertheless, I also found time to try out for every school play.

3. Use semicolons instead of commas to separate long, complicated items in a list.

Before: I studied biology in the ninth grade, geology in the tenth grade, chemistry—both organic and inorganic—in the eleventh grade, and physics, which became my very favorite subject, in the twelfth grade.

After: I studied biology in the ninth grade; geology in the tenth grade; chemistry–both organic and inorganic–in the eleventh grade; and physics, which became my very favorite subject, in the twelfth grade.

COLONS COUNT!

A colon signals that a list, definition, explanation, or concise summary of the part of the sentence before the colon is to follow. Here are three powerful writing rules about colons:

POWER LINE

The colon still serves well its pure role of bringing your sentence to a brief halt before you plunge into, say, a quotation or an itemized list.

–William Zinsser, *On Writing Well*

1. Make sure a colon follows a complete sentence. Often, some word or phrase reinforces the colon: "the following" or "as follows."

   Correct: The procedure was as follows: we began by observing the mice for thirty minutes without interruption.

   Correct: We made an important discovery: Left to their own devices, they were completely uninterested in running the maze.

2. Don't use a colon to separate parts of one sentence.

   Wrong: We needed: time, patience, and a stopwatch.

   Correct (list): This is what we needed: time, patience, and a stopwatch.

   Correct (summary): We needed very little: just time, patience, and a stopwatch.

3. Sometimes a colon, like a semicolon, links two complete sentences. A colon is used when the first sentence suggests or implies the second.

   Correct (explanation): We were astonished: The once-dull mice had become lively and even eager to run the maze.

Of course, you could also have used a period after *astonished*. The colon, though, helps emphasize the connection between the two sentences. It rushes the reader from one sentence to the next, whereas a period would signal a longer pause.

USE HYPHENS AND DASHES CORRECTLY

There are seven basic rules for hyphens and dashes. Don't try to memorize them! If you just look them over and try to stay awake, we'll be happy. If a rule seems hard to understand, just look at the examples, and you'll get it. And don't worry if, after Rule 3, your eyes start to glaze over. You know where these rules are and how to find them. Just use them on an "as-needed" basis.

POWER LINE

The hyphen can play tricks on the unwary as it did in Chattanooga when two newspapers merged—the News and Free Press. Someone introduced a hyphen into the merger, and the paper became the News-Free Press, which sounds as though the paper were news free or devoid of news.

—E. B. White

1. Use a hyphen when you have to break a word at the end of a line. Check a dictionary if you want to know where the word can be broken.

    Correct: For some time, I have been quite concerned about my daughter's lack of progress.

2. Use hyphens with compound numbers from twenty-one through ninety-nine, and with fractions used as adjectives—but not with fractions used as nouns.

    Correct: Although she scores in the ninety-fifth percentile on intelligence tests, her grades show that she is in the bottom two thirds of her class. (hyphen between "ninety" and "fifth"; no hyphen between "two" and "thirds" because "two thirds" is a noun)

    Correct: I understand a two-thirds vote of the faculty is needed to certify a child for special education.

3. Use hyphens with the prefixes *ex-*, *all-*, *self-*, and *semi-*, and with the suffix *-elect*.

   Correct: The school's ex-principal, Ms. Jorgenson, was a strong believer in student self-sufficiency, and she launched an all-out campaign to give students more independence.

   Correct: Mr. Samuels, the president-elect of the PTA, does not agree with her ideas.

4. Use a hyphen with a compound adjective when it comes before the word it modifies, but not when the same words are used as a noun.

   Correct (compound adjective): The no-holds-barred debate at the PTA meeting made many enemies for Mr. Samuels.

   Correct: The debate continued with no holds barred.

5. Use the hyphen to link any prefix with a proper noun or adjective.

   Correct (prefix with proper noun): The anti-PTA sentiments of some parents are rather disturbing.

   Correct (prefix with proper adjective): During the American Revolution, those who were pro-British were called "Tories."

6. Use a hyphen after a prefix when necessary to avoid confusion.

   Correct: We have decided to re-form our committee on special education. (re-form, not reform)

   Correct: We all need to be re-educated on this important issue. (Reeducated would sound and look funny!)

7. A dash should be used when you want to indicate an abrupt change of thought.

   Correct: Many children–including, of course, my own daughter–would benefit from such programs.

Correct: Teachers would also benefit from knowing more about special education–especially if they are given specific suggestions on how to apply these ideas in their classrooms.

In each example above, the words after the dash could have been put in parentheses, but that would have made them seem less important—as if they could be followed by the words, *by the way.* . . . So a dash is for parenthetical words that are too important to go in parentheses.

USE APOSTROPHES CORRECTLY

You'll be pleased to know that there are only two rules to keep in mind when using apostrophes—and after this, no more rules! Here are the two.

1. Use an apostrophe in a contraction. A *contraction* is a combination of two words with one or more letters left out. The apostrophe shows where the missing letters would be.

    Correct: You're asking for trouble! (you're = you are)

    Correct: Harry's got the biggest dog in town. (Harry's = Harry has)

    Correct: You'd love to meet him. (you'd = you would)

Be careful. Some possessive pronouns sound like contractions (for example, *your* and *its*, but they do not take apostrophes).

    Correct: Is this your gerbil? I'm looking for its owner.

Although we've used contractions throughout this text, that's just part of our charming, informal style. If you're writing fiction, a personal letter, or some other type of informal writing, use contractions with our blessing. But if you're doing formal or academic writing, be careful. Some professors and employers think that contractions don't belong in formal contexts. To play it safe, don't use them in formal writing.

2. Use apostrophes to show the possessive form of a noun. The general rule is that to form a singular possessive you add *'s*. To form a plural possessive, you add *s* or *es* to make the word plural, and then add an apostrophe at the end.

> **Correct (singular):** That is Julia's comb.
>
> **Correct (plural):** That is the boys' locker room.

Some plurals are irregular and don't take an s at the end: *women, children, men,* and *fish,* for example. To make these possessive, treat them as if they were singular and add *'s*.

> **Correct:** That's the children's school.

One last plural possessive problem: What do you do if someone's last name ends in s, and you want to make it both plural and possessive? In other words, what if you have friends named Terry and Kitty Wills, and you want to say you're going over to their house. First, make the name plural: the *Willses.* Then follow the rule for a plural possessive and add an apostrophe.

> **Correct:** I'm going over to the Willses' house.

Plug In

Here's your chance to polish. On the space provided, rewrite the following sentences, keeping these principles in mind:

- Be careful about how you use slang and colloquialisms.
- Beware of sentence fragments and run-on sentences.
- Use commas correctly.
- Use semicolons and colons correctly.
- Use hyphens and dashes correctly.
- Use apostrophes correctly.

Feel free to check back through this section if you're not sure how a rule should work. But also feel free to use your own eye and your own sense of rhythm, based on the reading and writing you've already done. Your goal is not just to memorize a set of rules, but to get a feel for how these details make writing more forceful and easier to understand.

The following sentences are from an interoffice memo (an imaginary one, of course). Keep in mind that you are working on a formal piece of business writing as you make your revisions. When you check your own revisions with ours, if you don't understand a change that's been made, look back through this chapter for an explanation.

1. Mr. Hodge really is an awfully good sales manager.

   _____

2. He has a nice way with his salespeople he also copes well with customers who might happen to complain.

   _____

3. And when it comes to drawing up year end projections! Theres just nobody better.

   _____

4. Two thirds of his staff have given him the highest possible tribute they havent missed a single day of work this year.

   _____

5. The rest of his staff is there at least eighty five percent of the time.

   _____

6. As a result his departments earnings have shown a one quarter increase a full 25 percent! in the last year alone.

_____

7. My recommendation? Lets give him a big bonus right away and then lets raise his salary by at least ten percent.

_____

8. Its about time we recognized good work in the clearest possible way, financially.

_____

9. I realize that this may cause some problems with personnel however I think we can talk them into it.

_____

10. At any rate, thats my recommendation. What's your's?

_____

Plug In Solutions

Here are our suggested revisions for the Plug In sentences:

1. Mr. Hodge is an excellent sales manager. (The revised sentence is more formal. The word *excellent*, we admit, is vague, but the rest of the memo goes into specifics.)
2. He has warm relations with salespeople, and he is good at handling customers who have complaints. (The language is pared down and more formal. The vague word *nice* has been changed. The sentence is no longer a run-on because we've added a comma + *and*, and deleted *also*.)

3. There's no one better than he at drawing up year-end projections. (The revised sentence is more formal. There is no sentence fragment. An apostrophe has been added to *There's*. A hyphen has been added to the compound adjective, *year-end*.)

4. Two thirds of his staff have given him the highest possible tribute: They haven't missed a single day of work this year. (A colon connects the two sentences, showing that the second one explains the term *the highest possible tribute*. Since *two thirds* isn't used as an adjective, it doesn't need a hyphen.)

5. The rest of his staff is there at least eighty-five percent of the time. (Numbers from twenty-one through ninety-nine always take a hyphen.)

6. As a result, his department's earnings have shown a one-quarter increase—a full 25 percent—in the last year alone. (An apostrophe has been added to the possessive noun *department's*. One-quarter is hyphenated because it is used as an adjective. The dashes set off a parenthetical phrase, too important to be enclosed in parentheses.)

7. I recommend giving him the largest possible bonus and raising his salary by at least ten percent. (*I recommend* . . . is more formal than *let's*. The sentence fragment has been eliminated.)

8. Perhaps if we reward good work by financial rewards, more employees will be motivated to put forth their best efforts. (The original sentence was gibberish. We fixed it. In the process, we got rid of *Its*, a contraction without an apostrophe. You may have made different choices that were equally acceptable.)

9. I realize that this may cause some problems with personnel; however, I think we can convince them to agree. (We got rid of the *it* at the end, which didn't refer to anything. If you're not sure why we added the semicolon, check back through the chapter.)

10. In any case, that's my recommendation. I look forward to hearing yours. (We added an apostrophe to the contraction *that's*. The tone is considerably more formal, although we did throw caution to the wind and leave the contraction in. You may have changed it to *that is* . . . Finally, we deleted the apostrophe in *yours* because it is a possessive pronoun, not a contraction.)

BEFORE YOU CONTINUE

If you polished these sentences to your own satisfaction, move on to Section Two, where you'll finally get to do some writing. If you missed more than three or four of the corrections, especially those concerning punctuation, you might want to go over those rules again. Even if you did have trouble with this "writing rules" section, you can certainly go on to focus on other aspects of writing. The rules will always be here waiting whenever you want to think about them again. Now that you've gotten through this material, think of it as a handy, powerful writing reference to use if you run into trouble.

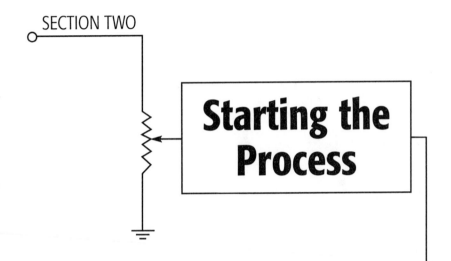

Starting the Process

Get Yourself Organized

We'll repeat our earlier remarks about writing: Writing is often like running a race, and you need to think about the stages of writing and where writing fits in with your individual plans, strengths, and weaknesses. We focused on a lot of rules for good writing in Section One, and in this second section, we'll focus on the writing process itself. Let's go through a few ways to get yourself more organized and ready for powerful writing.

Warming Up. Try a few of the brainstorming exercises included in Section Two. Get your mind thinking, creating, and trying some new ways of writing.

Stretching. Once you have some ideas, or feel that you know exactly what you want to write about, try extending your thoughts on this topic. Use the chapter on developing ideas (chapter 6) to help you do this.

Working Out. Once you get a topic that you know you want to expand, and you have tried some methods of doing this, begin to shape it, order it, hone it down.

Training. You may have to try a few different ways of ordering your work. Stick with it. The order you want will become clear as you try different techniques.

Sprint. Find that concise, clear thesis statement. If you can fit it on a 3 by 5 index card, then it is about the length you want. Use charts and diagrams, drawings and outlines to figure out exactly what kind of writing you are going to produce in relation to this thesis statement.

Marathon. Make a formal outline of your topic. Look at the ones provided as examples and go from there.

Cooling Down. Before going on, show your outline to someone and ask them to let you know if it is clear. Redo it if there are some parts that do not seem to follow logically.

Personal Best. Let your outline sit for a day or two. Go back to it. Make any changes you see after looking at it from a fresh viewpoint. Then go on and begin drafting!

TUNE IN TO THE PROCESS

There are some things that some people can do and others just can't—like making your ears wiggle, or touching the tip of your nose with the tip of your tongue. Writing isn't one of those things. It's not even like having a photographic memory, or being able to multiply two five-digit numbers in your head. It's an ordinary skill that can be learned, like most skills, step by step, and with practice.

Before going any further, let's get something straight. When we say *writing*, we are not talking about writing lyric poetry or the great American novel. Those kinds of writing take special talent . . . and you may indeed have it! But in this book, when we say *writing*, we mean practical writing: letters, essays, reports—any kind of writing people use to communicate information or ideas. Keeping this sense of the word *writing* in mind, get your self-confidence into high gear. This section of the book is going to take you through the writing process, step by step, from getting started through the finished product.

Thinking before writing, like looking before leaping, can make your life a lot easier. For example, does your heart sink an inch or two when you have to write? Even seasoned writers experience sinking-heart syndrome. Usually it is because they don't know what to write about, or even if they do, they just can't seem to get started.

POWER LINE

The very first thing I tell my new students on the first day of a workshop is that good writing is about telling the truth. We are a species that needs and wants to understand who we are. Sheep lice do not seem to share this longing, which is one reason they write so very little. But we do. We have so much we want to say and figure out.

—Anne Lamott, *Bird By Bird*

This section will take you through the first steps of the writing process—the thinking and planning that let you get on with your writing while keeping your heart in the right place. You'll learn some simple techniques for finding and narrowing down your topic and getting your ideas organized, so that when you're ready to write, you'll already know what you plan to say and how you plan to say it. When you come to Section Three, you'll be ready to leap right in.

CHAPTER FIVE

○Finding a Topic

Why are you writing? If your answer to this question is "because I have to," take a deep breath and think again. Even if you're writing a book report for a homework assignment or an essay for a college application, your writing does have a purpose. And getting that purpose straight in your head is step one of the thinking phase.

KNOW YOUR PURPOSE

Here are just some of the possible purposes for writing. You can write to:

- Instruct—You have to explain to fellow office members how to use the new coffeemaker.

- Inform—Your boss wants you to write a report telling what you've accomplished at the end of each month.

- Make a request—You've been getting billed for a subscription to *Iguana Monthly,* and you don't even own an iguana. You want the magazine to stop billing you—and to stop sending the magazine.

- Persuade—You want to persuade your assemblyman to vote against the bill to eliminate rent control, and remind him that many voters in your district think the same way.

- Express feelings—Uncle Eduardo hasn't forgotten your birthday since your very first one. He sent you a CD for this birthday, and you want to let him know you appreciate it—and him.

- Express ideas—You're writing a term paper about the causes of World War I for your history class.

In many practical, real-world writing situations, you know your topic before you even begin thinking about your purpose and your audience. But you may encounter situations in which you need to find a topic for your writing. Here are some such situations, just for starters:

∿∿ **POWER LINE** ∿∿

When I sit at my table to write, I never know what it's going to be until I am underway. I trust in inspiration which sometimes comes and sometimes doesn't. But I don't sit back waiting for it. I work every day.

—Alberto Moravia

- That letter to your niece. You want to write to her, but you don't know what to say to a nine-year-old girl, particularly since you haven't been nine yourself for quite a while now.

- Your teacher gives you an assignment that goes, "Write an essay about a personal experience," or even worse, "Write an essay."

- You have a pile of blank college applications on your desk, and each one of them wants you to "Write an essay" about something or other—an experience that has had a major impact on your life, a person you admire, a book you enjoyed reading.

- A job application has a page with lots of blank lines on it and one sentence at the top: "Tell more about yourself in the space provided."

- Your boss asks you to "say a few words" at the next sales meeting.

If you find yourself having to write but not knowing what to write about, this section is for you. Here are some ideas for getting ideas.

TAKE A PERSONAL INTEREST INVENTORY

This technique is especially good for people who will be filling out applications for college, grad school, or internship programs, all of which tend to ask a lot of very general questions about who you are. So who are you? What moves you? What makes you mad? What intrigues you? You will do your best writing if you choose a topic that you sincerely care about.

Your Turn

On a separate sheet of paper, complete the following sentences. See if writing as a response to them sparks any ideas.

1. In my spare time, I _____.

2. My ideal job would be _____.

3. Something that really annoyed me recently was _____.

4. I've never been able to understand why _____.

5. The best movie I've ever seen was _____. I loved it because _____.

6. The best book I've ever read was _____. I loved it because _____.

7. A book/movie/TV show I dislike is _____, because _____.

8. I've always wanted to visit _____, where I would _____.

9. My favorite music is _____, because when I hear it, I _____.

You get the idea. Create your own sentences to complete. These sentences can be about sports, hobbies, nature, favorite vacations you've taken, ideal vacations you'd like to take, qualities in people you admire, faults in people you can't stand, and so on. Notice the topics to which you have strong responses, either positive or negative. Somewhere in that strong response is an idea you really care about, an idea you'd like to communicate to others—in other words, the raw material for a good piece of writing.

Keep a Journal. A journal is really a place to collect material that could some day be turned into writing ideas. If you decide to keep a journal, you might want to carry a small notebook around wherever you go. When something strikes your fancy, write it down. Don't worry about grammar, spelling, or even writing full sentences—just put down whatever will jog your memory. Bring back the thought, experience, or sense impression you thought worth recording. Some people who keep journals write in them just once at the end of the day. Either way, the result is a book full of writing ideas.

> **POWER LINE**
>
> "I don't know where to start," one [student] will wail. Start with your childhood, I tell them. Plug your nose and jump in, and write down all your memories as truthfully as you can.
>
> —Anne Lamott, *Bird by Bird*

Your Turn

On a separate piece of paper, try writing about one of these:

- An idea you have for doing something in a better way
- Something you wonder about
- A memory that pops into your head
- Something you notice that's especially beautiful/ugly/funny
- Something you hear—or overhear
- Something you read about in the newspaper or see on TV

When you're jotting down your ideas, you may not see how any of them could possibly become great essays. Most of them may not—but some will. When you are faced with one of those "Write an essay about . . ." or "Tell us something about . . ." assignments, go to your journal or your notes. Read through what you've jotted down for ideas. You're likely to find one or more.

KEEP A CLIPPINGS FILE

Start collecting articles from newspapers and magazines. These might be on topics that interest you, such as gun control or a favorite actor. Perhaps what catches your interest is a moment of humor, irony, or emotion. An article might include a quote that moves you; a review of a bad movie might contain a clever put-down that you really enjoyed; a cartoon might strike you as particularly amusing.

Some people find it useful to highlight or underline the bits of an article that affected them most. Others like to write comments in the margins, "talking back" to the article. Then, when it comes time to find an essay topic, they just continue the conversation.

Photographs, advertisements, and even junk mail might go into your file. Save whatever catches your fancy, and come back to it later when you're looking for ideas.

FREEWRITING

Freewriting means writing down whatever comes to your mind. Say you've been given the assignment, "Tell us about a person who influenced you." Write "People Who Influenced Me" at the top of a page, and plunge in. Commit to writing for a specific length of time, say 15 minutes (or five, if 15 sounds too daunting), and keep those little fingers moving without stopping. Don't "self-censor" what you write. No one will ever read it, and you can toss it after it's served its purpose. Here's one writer's freewrite:

POWER LINE

And then the miracle happens. The sun comes up again. So you get up and do your morning things, and one thing leads to another, and eventually, at nine, you find yourself back at the desk, staring blankly at the pages you filled yesterday. And there on page four is a paragraph with all sorts of life in it, smells and sounds and voices and colors and even a moment of dialogue that makes you say to yourself, very, very, softly, 'hmmm.'

—Anne Lamott, *Bird by Bird*

People Who Influenced Me

Mom, when I was young . . . going off to work. Looked great. She liked her job. Aunt Lydia and Uncle Dave. They were always so happy. Lydia: "Do what you love and the rest will follow." Dave: "But be sure you have money in the bank!" Money in the bank. What do I have there right now? I can't even balance my checkbook! Math. Mr. Jenkins, math teacher. I certainly hate math. Is that his fault? He was so boring. Bald spot. Glasses. Yelling at Barry Barton. Poor Barry. I would never be that kind of teacher. Ms. Garwood, pink eyeglasses, white hair. Great teacher. OK, enough of that. Who else influenced me? Roberto Suarez, I admired him because he never gave up. I remember the time he was almost failing— what? math? No, social studies. And he got into an argument with the teacher. He said . . . .

[The freewriting keeps going on for another ten minutes or so.]

Clearly, freewriting is *for your eyes only*. Because it's so personal and spontaneous, it might help you unlock an idea or two. Our freewriter—let's call him Malcolm—might find himself writing about his mother, Mr. Jenkins, Ms. Garwood, Roberto Suarez, or some other character who emerges in the freewrite—people he may not have thought about in years. Yet, as he writes, he finds himself remembering people, incidents, and conversations that might become the focus for an essay.

How can you turn your sprawling freewrite into a tightly constructed essay? Don't worry about that now. At the moment, your job is simply to find a topic that gets you going.

KNOW YOUR AUDIENCE

Knowing your audience means getting a handle on your readers. So who are your readers? Are you writing for a possible employer, a school admissions committee, a dear friend, a friendly office staff, a hostile office staff?

Let's say your audience is Mr. Skeffington, the circulation manager of *Iguana Monthly*. Your purpose is to get him to stop billing you for a magazine you never subscribed to. But who is this mysterious Mr. Skeffington? Will he be more receptive to threats ("If this isn't cleared up in ten business days, I'll sue!") or flattery ("I realize you have many accounts to monitor . . . ")?

Visualizing your audience helps you decide what tone to take and what facts to include ("I have already consulted with my attorney, and he tells me . . . "). It also helps get you in the mood for writing. Now you're committed: You have someone you're trying to reach. If you're writing for people you actually know—family, friends, co-workers—picture one or more of them as you think about your topic. Even if you're writing for people you've never met, like an admissions committee, a prospective employer, or the mysterious Mr. Skeffington, we still advise you to visualize your audience.

Use available information plus your knowledge of the world to imagine your reader. Is he or she old or young, dressed in a suit or sweats, understanding or inflexible? Ask yourself what your readers want to hear, what they need to hear, and what you want to tell them. Thinking about who's going to read your work makes it easier to get your thoughts in order.

Take Mr. Skeffington, for example. You don't know him, he doesn't know you. Your business with each other is purely formal. Right there, you've got some hints about how your writing should look and sound. You'll use a formal business-letter form, rather than friendly-letter form; you'll begin your letter with "Dear Mr. Skeffington:" rather than, "Dear Al,"; you'll sign it "Very truly yours," or "Sincerely," rather than "Love," or "Your pal." Furthermore, your tone will be courteous and formal. You won't use contractions—that is, you will not use contractions.

On the other hand, if you were writing a letter to your nine-year-old niece, you'd use the friendly-letter form, and you'd probably try to make your writing as much like casual speech as possible. You might also try to make your tone and content humorous at times, to capture your young relative's attention and make your letter more enjoyable for her to read.

FELICIA FINDS A TOPIC

In this section we will follow a fictitious high school student, Felicia, through the first part of her writing journey. We will continue to find out how she is doing as this section goes along.

She has to write one of those open-ended essays—"Tell us more about yourself in 250–500 words"—for her application to Ideal College.

Felicia starts *by thinking about her purpose:* She wants to persuade the Ideal admissions committee that she's the ideal student for them. What does that mean exactly? They already know about her grades and her SAT scores, so she doesn't have to repeat that information. There was a section on the application to describe extracurricular activities, so she's already mentioned her term on the student council, her three years playing bassoon in the school orchestra, her volunteer work as a candy striper, and her part-time job at a local bakery. (Felicia is a busy person.) She imagines that at least ten or fifteen thousand other busy students have put down pretty much the same things.

Then Felicia *thinks about her audience and tries to visualize them.* She "sees" a group of people, possibly even busier than herself, whose job it is to read those ten or fifteen thousand applications. They're looking for responsible, intelligent students, sure, but they're probably also sick of reading essays. And all those essays are starting to sound pretty much the same. She imagines they'll appreciate something unusual, maybe even a little funny—and short. (Also, by the way, typed or legibly written.)

Based on these thoughts, Felicia *refines her purpose:* She wants to persuade the committee to accept her by telling something unusual about herself. At this point, Felicia might take a personal interest inventory, look in her journal, consult her clipping file, or freewrite to find ideas. Being something of an overachiever, she does all four.

Among her *personal interests,* Felicia notes that she loves the beach. She considers writing about her feelings for nature, but that topic is hardly unusual. Maybe a description of the time she saw the Northern Lights, how mysterious and awe-inspiring they were? A possibility.

KAPLAN

In her *journal*, Felicia finds several entries about her harrowing audition to move up from second to first bassoon. That story might make a good essay, and it says a lot about her: She was scared, but she worked through her fear; she was determined, practicing for hours; and she won, which shows she's a winner—always a nice quality in a college applicant.

In her *clippings file*, Felicia finds the review of a movie that she just couldn't stand. The movie was violent, which the reviewer loved and Felicia hated. "Maybe I should write about why I hate violence in the movies," Felicia thinks. She could talk both about how movie violence affects society and about how she herself is affected by it, so the committee gets a sense of both her opinions and her personality.

Then Felicia *freewrites for fifteen minutes* on the topic, "What I want people to know about me." She finds herself writing about what she doesn't want people to know about her—that sometimes she's insecure, doesn't know what she's doing, is clumsy, feels awkward. In fact, that was exactly how she felt the first time she took t'ai chi, a Chinese martial art that Felicia has been studying at the local Y. She's such a beginner that she didn't even mention t'ai chi among her extracurricular activities. Somehow, she feels moved to write about it now.

Felicia doesn't exactly know how her essay will turn out. But she feels intrigued by this idea, and she's willing to give it a try. If this topic doesn't work out, I can always start over with one of the others, she tells herself. So for now, Felicia has found a topic: "What I've Learned from Studying T'ai Chi."

Plug In

Now it's your turn. Choose one of the following two situations to practice creating a topic:

- You have to write 250–500 words (one to two typewritten, double-spaced pages) on a topic of your choice for a college or job application. Choose a topic.
- You have to speak for five minutes (about two doubled-spaced pages' worth of talking) on some topic related to your job. You will be giving this speech at a company-wide gathering—a sales meeting, a company

picnic, an awards dinner, or a "get to know you" meeting with new management. Decide exactly where you might be giving this speech and then choose a topic.

Here's some help. Ask yourself:

- "What is my purpose?"
- "Who is my audience?"
- "Why do they want or need to know what I have to tell them?"

If you don't have a journal or clippings file to go to (you mean you didn't start them already?), take a personal inventory or freewrite. See what you come up with.

Good luck! Once you've chosen a topic, join us in the next chapter as we discuss how to develop your ideas.

KAPLAN

CHAPTER SIX

○ Developing Ideas

So now you've got your general topic. What are you going to say about it? Read on to find out about some techniques your fellow writers have found helpful in developing their ideas about a writing topic.

ASK QUESTIONS

Reporters have to answer six questions they call "the Five Ws and H": Who? What? When? Where? Why? How?

These are great questions for you to ask yourself about your topic. For example, let's return to our friend Malcolm, the one who freewrote about "People Who Influenced Me." As a result of that freewrite, he decided to write about Roberto Suarez, his old school buddy. Here's how Malcolm used questions to flesh out his thoughts:

Q: *Who* influenced me?

A: Roberto Suarez.

Q: *What* did he do that was so important?

A: Argued with social studies teacher, even though he was failing . . . wouldn't back down . . . said we should be learning about Mexico . . . Teacher: "Okay, do report!" Roberto turned in 20-page paper, got an A.

Q: *When* did this happen?

A: Seventh grade

Q: *Where* did this happen?

A: That was when we still lived in Glenwood, California.

Q: *Why* did this impress me so much?

A: I thought Roberto was pretty dumb—I was wrong. He was really smart. Had guts. I learned that people can surprise you. Also—if you stick up for what you believe in, you can make a difference.

Q: *How* has this affected me?

A: Two ways: Made me more ready to stand up for myself. Made me less quick to judge people in a negative way.

As you can see, Malcolm isn't worried how his writing sounds or looks; he's just trying to clarify his own thoughts and to remember as much as possible about a particular experience. He might end up writing about one of the two ways in which the Roberto incident influenced him. He might even end up writing about the need for more multicultural studies in the school curriculum. You'll find out later.

READ AND TAKE NOTES

Sometimes it's hard to get started on a topic. Maybe you really don't know enough, particularly if you're writing a research paper or a report on a specialized topic. Or perhaps you do know enough but still want a boost from an outside source. You might want to know how another writer has handled the same topic. Maybe you're just lonely for the sound of another writer's voice.

In these cases, read and take notes to develop your ideas. For hints on doing research, skip ahead and check out the chapter on reports. That's where you'll learn how to find books on your topic. Then come back here and try one or more of these techniques:

- As you read, *jot down any details or ideas* that strike you as being interesting or useful. Note the title, author, and page number so you can come back to it if necessary.

- At key points—the ends of sections or chapters, for example—*write down the main idea* of what you've just read. Respond to what you've read by noting questions, thoughts, and opinions that may have occurred to you.

- *Take notes on index cards.* That way you can shuffle them around and put thoughts on the same subject together. Again, write the title, author, and page number of the book on each card.

BRAINSTORM

Brainstorming is like a game you play with another person or by yourself. The object is to come up with as many thoughts as possible on a topic. If you were looking for a fancier term, you might call it "free association." Here are some trusted brainstorming techniques.

> ○‿₩₩‿○ **POWER LINE** ○‿₩₩‿○
>
> For exploratory stages or for trying to untangle a fuzzy thought, I have found that I invariably return to pen and writing pad. Experiment with various writing tools until you find the medium that helps your thoughts flow most freely. In the end, you must do what feels right for you.
>
> —Gabriele Rico,
> *Writing the Natural Way*

Brainstorm with Others

With a trusted friend, family member, or colleague, toss around ideas on the topic you have chosen. This is obviously a more useful technique for less personal topics. And you need to make sure that your brainstorming partner(s) won't object to your using any or all ideas from the session, regardless of who came up with them first. Make sure someone—probably you!—is taking notes. The object: Say and then write down all the ideas you can possibly think of on a topic, with no judgment or evaluation allowed.

Joshua, a personnel director for a small company, has to speak for five minutes at a monthly employees' meeting on the topic "How to Improve Employee Morale." He asks two fellow employees, Ray and Gloria, to get together to toss around some ideas on the topic:

Ray: Something that really bothers me is that our schedule is so rigid. Like if your kids are late for school, or if you need something delivered to your house–too bad. You've still got to be here at 9:00.

Gloria: I agree, but how could the office run with everyone just coming in any time they want?

Joshua: You know, I have a friend who works for this company that lets everyone work at home a certain number of hours each month. They just have to have a computer with a modem connected to the office. They call it "Home Work."

Ray: I know someone who works in an office where they have "emergency days" in addition to "personal days."

And so on. If the brainstorming session continues in this direction, Joshua might come up with working at home part time as one of the ways to improve company morale. He'd probably come up with some other ways, too.

Brainstorm by Yourself

If you don't have brainstorming buddies, or if you'd rather work alone, you can still brainstorm. Just set yourself to listing as many ideas as possible about your topic. Again, don't censor or evaluate.

Jocelyn, a personnel director for a different company, had to write a memo on the topic, "How to Reduce Employee Turnover." She started by brainstorming:

1. Offer day care

2. Expand vacation–one week per year, four weeks/four years (ten weeks/ten years?)

3. More promotions

4. Offer flex-time (more flexibility in working hours)

5. Do employee survey–find out more about why people leave

6. Lunch at fancy restaurant on year anniversary

7. Training? back-to-school programs?

8. Build an employee gym

9. Two more personal days after five years

Note how some of Jocelyn's ideas are realistic, some are fantastic, and some are just not well thought out. That's okay. What's important for now is that she has ideas. How she will select and organize her ideas later on will be important, as well.

MAKE AN IDEA CLUSTER OR WORD WEB

An idea cluster, also known as a "word web," helps you generate ideas by showing how one idea leads to another. To make a cluster, write your topic in the center of a page and draw a circle around it. Jot down related words or phrases, circle them, and use lines to connect them to the general topic. Keep writing related words and phrases until you've said everything you have to say, at least for the moment.

Like Malcolm, Margarita has to write an essay on "A Person Who Influenced Me." She's decided to write about her grandmother. Here's the cluster she made to develop her ideas:

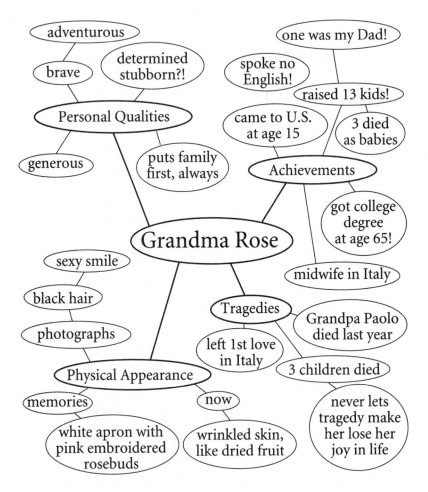

Notice how Margarita let each idea in her cluster lead her on to more ideas. When she wrote "physical appearance," for example, she started to describe her grandmother, then realized that she had two different images of her: how she looks now and how Margarita remembers her. That in turn provoked her to remember photographs of Grandma Rose, taken long before Margarita ever knew her.

Likewise, writing about her grandmother's raising 13 kids, which she entered under "achievements," reminded Margarita of the three children who died. This inspired Margarita to start a new category, "tragedies."

TRY FOCUSED FREEWRITING

Focused freewriting is much like just plain freewriting. The difference is that you already have a topic, so you don't just let your mind wander freely, but keep it focused on that topic. By writing anything and everything that comes into your head about your topic, it's almost a sure bet that you'll discover ideas you never even knew you had. In fact, focused freewriting is a good trick to keep up your sleeve at any point in the writing process when your mind just gets stuck. It's an amazingly great way to get those little wheels up there turning again.

FELICIA DEVELOPS HER IDEAS

The journey of Felicia's writing continues. When we last left her, she had her topic—"What I've Learned from T'ai Chi"—for her college application. She asked questions about her topic, relying on the "Five W's and H"; she read up more on t'ai chi; she used brainstorming or clustering techniques, as well. Finally, Felicia used focused freewriting to develop her ideas about her experiences with t'ai chi. Here's part of what she wrote. Notice how, when she gets stuck, she keeps repeating words over and over until a new idea comes. Remember, the idea of freewriting is to keep writing *without stopping!*

What I've Learned Studying T'ai Chi

Remember to tell them what t'ai chi is—Chinese martial art, self-defense (physical), mental discipline, emotional strength. Okay, but what have I learned? learned learned learned It's hard. Sometimes hard work pays off. What else? What else? What else? Feeling physically stronger has boosted my self-confidence. What about the mental part? Concentrating when I practice helps me concentrate on other things too—like studying. They'd like to hear that! What about the time I was yelled at by the teacher? He said, "You must have patience." I was so embarrassed. In school, I'm used to being the best in the class. He said, "The brain must learn from the body." Didn't understand. Didn't know what to do. Wanted to quit, but I didn't. That's good, too! Instead, I practiced harder. My teacher said, "Not so bad. Now work more!" Later, he gave a speech. "When you ask, why am I not the best?, that's not modest. There is always someone better. Maybe you're very smart. There is always someone smarter." So I learned how to keep going even when I didn't think I was very good. That's the emotional strength part.

Like the other writers we've met in this section, Felicia has gotten to know more about her own thoughts, feelings, and experiences as they relate to her topic.

Plug In

Time to show off your writing power! Take the topic you've chosen for your essay or speech (see your Plug In exercise material from chapter 5) and develop your ideas further. Use one or more of the techniques in this section. Remember, you have many ways to choose from:

- Ask questions
- Read and take notes
- Brainstorm with others
- Brainstorm by yourself
- Make an idea cluster or word web
- Try focused freewriting

CHAPTER SEVEN

Narrowing Your Topic

Now that you have developed some ideas about your topic, it is possible that you have chosen an idea on which to focus. But it is also possible that your topic is just too big for the amount of writing or speaking you're

planning to do. For example, Felicia wants to write about what she's learned from t'ai chi, and she's got some ideas about what she wants to say, but she's learned so much. People write whole books on what's to be learned from the martial arts. Now is the time for Felicia to narrow her topic—to find one aspect of that topic that is manageable for a 250–500 word essay rather than a 300-page book. Let's leave Felicia to her narrowing-down work while we look at some other examples.

BEING BRIEF: TWO ESSAY PATTERNS

The pitfalls of a too-broad topic are obvious. If you have to write 250–500 words (about two typewritten, double-spaced pages) about "someone who influenced you," you don't have time or space to write an entire biography. This is just about what you've got time for:

- One paragraph to identify the person (my tenth-grade woodworking teacher) and describe the person briefly (tall, skinny, in his early 40s, shining eyes and long, tapered fingers)

- Three or four paragraphs to tell one story about how the person affected you (the time he stayed after class for an hour, until you finally learned how to use a lathe)
- One paragraph to make clear exactly why this incident was so important (it taught you perseverance and a willingness to work hard)

Of course, you could always go about writing your short essay another way. Here's our second brief essay suggestion:

- One paragraph to tell how your teacher studied woodworking in Germany and Japan
- One paragraph to describe the beautiful bowls, statues, and birdhouses he sold to local galleries
- Three or four paragraphs to tell about the day you spent in his workshop, watching him turn an ordinary block of wood into a thing of beauty and a joy forever
- One final paragraph to explain that he inspired you, too, to become an artist

The focus of the first essay would be: "How I learned the importance of hard work from my woodworking teacher." The focus of the second essay would be: "How my woodworking teacher inspired me to become an artist."

There's room to do one essay or the other. But in two pages, there isn't room for both. What if your teacher inspired you both to work hard and to become an artist? Sorry, Charlie. You've only got two pages. You'll have to choose. Here are some ways to narrow your topic down to one that's just right for Goldilocks: not too big, not too small, but just right.

SUBDIVIDE YOUR TOPIC

Remember our earlier example of speaking for five minutes about employee morale? In a brainstorming session, one of the ideas Joshua and his colleagues came up with was allowing employees to work a certain number of hours at home. They also came up with the idea of "emergency days." Those are both good ideas, but Joshua would need more than five minutes to go into detail about either one. Joshua chose "Working at Home," but even that topic seemed too broad for a five-minute talk. He broke the topic down into its component parts and then wrote about only one of the parts.

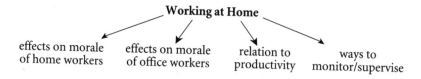

Working at Home

effects on morale of home workers   effects on morale of office workers   relation to productivity   ways to monitor/supervise

Begin Narrowing Your Topic

Ask questions! Some people narrow a topic by asking themselves a series of progressively narrower questions. You can make this method even more clear by using a graphic aid, such as an inverted triangle.

For example, Ralph has to write a ten-page term paper for his course in Victorian history. Using a combination of brainstorming and freewriting, he has determined that what interests him most is Victorian women. But this topic is still far too broad. So he uses questions to narrow his topic.

POWER LINE

The poet is the unsatisfied child who dares to ask the difficult question which arises from the schoolmaster's answer to his simple question, and the then still more difficult question which arises from that.

—Robert Graves

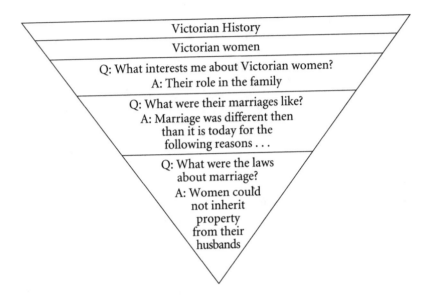

Victorian History

Victorian women

Q: What interests me about Victorian women?
A: Their role in the family

Q: What were their marriages like?
A: Marriage was different then
than it is today for the
following reasons . . .

Q: What were the laws
about marriage?
A: Women could
not inherit
property
from their
husbands

Focused Topic: How were Victorian women affected by the marriage laws of the time?

Notice how Ralph uses each question to focus the topic more and more narrowly. He could keep going. For example, he could ask about different kinds of wives: the industrialist middle-class, aristocratic, and working-class wives. Then he would choose one type to write about. Or he might choose a smaller time period, focusing on, say, the year a particular law was passed rather than on the whole Victorian era. How does he know when to stop? He stops when he thinks his topic is narrow enough to be adequately covered in the space he is allowed.

EXAMINE TOPICS FROM DIFFERENT PERSPECTIVES

You can also narrow your topic by looking at it from many different angles. Write the topic in the center of a page. Around that center, identify the different approaches you might take. Here's how Ruth narrowed down a topic for the essay she wrote for social studies class:

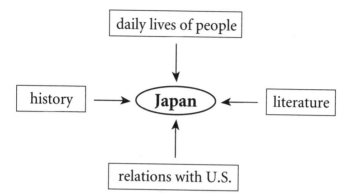

If Ruth needs to narrow her topic still further, she can ask herself key questions that refine the topic from a variety of perspectives:

- *How* have United States–Japanese relations changed over the years?
- *When* did the most important changes take place?
- *Why* have they changed?

These questions can help Ruth come up with a focused topic that both interests her and will be manageable to research and write.

FELICIA NARROWS HER TOPIC

The last time we left her, Felicia had used focused freewriting. From this freewriting, she discovered many ideas about what she'd learned from t'ai chi. Now she finds that she can *subdivide* t'ai chi into three different categories: physical, intellectual, and emotional. She finds that the idea that is most compelling for her comes under "emotional strength": learning to keep trying, even in the face of failure. She will continue by using this as her topic.

Plug In

Think about your topic from earlier exercises, and the ideas you've developed. Maybe your topic is just right for a 250–500 word essay. If so, fine. But think it over. Consider the following questions:

- Will you really be able to cover your topic adequately, or will you just scratch its surface?
- Could you do a better job if you concentrated on just one aspect of your topic?

To help you narrow your topic, think about:

- Different essay patterns
- Subdividing your topic
- Asking questions
- Looking at your topic from different perspectives

Try one of these techniques and see if you come up with a smaller but more manageable topic to write about. But don't narrow down your topic too much, either. If Felicia made this mistake, she could end up going on and on about one incident so trivial that nobody really cares about it.

CHAPTER EIGHT

Writing a Thesis Statement

Once you have identified a topic of a manageable size, your next step is to write a "thesis statement." Don't let the fancy term fool you. A thesis statement is just one or two sentences that sum up the point you want to make.

DEVELOP A THESIS STATEMENT

Margarita, assigned to write on "Someone Who Influenced Me," chose the following thesis statement: "My grandmother has influenced me because she never let tragedy interfere with her joy in life." Malcolm, writing on the same topic, developed this thesis: "By questioning a decision made by an authority figure, Roberto Suarez influenced me by teaching me to stand up for what I believe in."

As you can see, a thesis statement *identifies your writing purpose and defines your point of view.* A clear, concise thesis can make your writing task far easier. Granted, it can be hard to focus all your thoughts into a single sentence, but take it from us—you'll be glad you did.

A thesis statement is like a compass needle: it literally helps to keep you on course. At every point during your writing process you can pause and ask yourself, "Now how does this relate to my thesis?" Then you can bend your writing efforts to show how your point proves, clarifies, or otherwise illuminates your main idea.

CURB YOUR WANDERING WRITING

Sometimes you can find yourself spending half a page discussing an idea that *doesn't* relate to your thesis. In that case, you have two choices:

- Cross out the half page of writing and get back on track
- Revise your thesis statement, which will probably mean going back to square one

For example, the student who chose to write about his woodworking teacher wrote the thesis statement, "My woodworking teacher influenced my life by teaching me the value of hard work." Listen in on his thoughts when he finds himself writing about things that don't support that thesis:

> I've written a whole paragraph on my woodworking teacher's love of beauty. There's nothing in that paragraph that supports my thesis statement. I'd better cross out that paragraph and get back to my topic. But wait a minute. I think I changed my mind, and what I really want to focus on is how my teacher's love of beauty influenced me to become an artist. I guess it's back to the drawing board. I need a new thesis statement. How about, "My woodworking teacher influenced my life by teaching me that I am really an artist."

Use a Thesis Statement in Your Writing. Here's one of the most frequently asked questions regarding the thesis: Does a thesis statement have to actually appear in every essay? Our answer: Maybe. Maybe not. It depends.

You might *begin* your essay with your thesis statement: "My woodworking teacher, Mr. Maddox, influenced my life by teaching me that I am an artist." Or you might *end* with it: " . . . and that has changed my life." Your thesis statement might even wind up in the *middle* of your essay: "That's when I discovered my identity as an artist."

Or perhaps you won't ever come right out with your thesis statement; perhaps you'll write your essay in such a way that your audience gets your message without your ever stating it directly. You can decide all that when you're writing and revising (i.e., when you're up to the next sections). For now, just concentrate on knowing what your thesis is.

FELICIA FINDS A THESIS

When we last left Felicia, she had just narrowed her topic to "How my experiences with t'ai chi taught me to keep trying, even in the face of failure." Here's what she came up with for a thesis statement:

> T'ai chi has taught me to keep trying, even if I think I might fail.

Now when Felicia begins to write, she'll make sure that everything she includes helps demonstrate how and why learning t'ai chi has made her more persistent in her efforts to succeed, even if she's not the best in the class. Her thesis will help her focus her thoughts and direct her energies. And that's the power behind the thesis statement!

Plug In

Is it your turn already? Yes, it is. On a separate sheet of paper, use any of the techniques we've described in this chapter to write a thesis statement for your topic:

- Identify your purpose
- Define your point of view
- Revise your thesis if necessary
- Decide where to place the thesis in your essay

Hint: Make sure your thesis is narrow enough to cover a topic in the time and space allotted—but not too narrow.

CHAPTER NINE

Organizing Your Ideas

Now is it time to write? Nope. Not yet. Sure, you know your main idea. But now you have to get all your *supporting ideas* together. Supporting ideas support, or help make a case for, your thesis statement.

POWER LINE

But in most cases planning must be a deliberate prelude to writing. The first principle of composition, therefore, is to foresee or determine the shape of what is to come and pursue that shape.

—E. B. White

THINK ABOUT YOUR SUPPORTING IDEAS

Time to make a bold and sweeping statement: Every single idea in your essay should, in some way, make a case for your thesis statement. That's right, and we're not exaggerating. *Every single idea.*

Your Turn

You may already have all your supporting ideas in your head. As a test to find out, try this exercise:

1. Write your thesis statement at the top of a page.
2. Ask yourself exactly what you want to say to support it, or make your case.
3. List four or five supporting ideas that seem clear and relevant to you.

If you can list four or five ideas that you feel will make your case, you are ready to go on to the next chapter, "Putting Your Ideas in Order." But if you are even the least bit concerned that you might be missing something, hang out in this chapter for a while longer.

To help you write powerfully, we will suggest several graphic organizers to get your supporting ideas together. Oops—there goes another term that may need defining. A *graphic organizer* is a pattern or form you draw on a sheet of paper that helps get your supporting ideas together. An idea cluster or word web is an example of a graphic organizer. Read on to learn about some more. They can really be quite helpful!

MAKE AN ANALYSIS FRAME

Different kinds of writing require different kinds of graphic organizers. An *analysis frame*, for example, can help you write a:

- Response to a work of literature
- Review of a book, play, or movie
- Comparative analysis—an essay that analyzes two different items (for example, two works of literature or two different historical periods)

To make an analysis frame, *identify the elements* you'll need to prove your thesis: character, setting, plot; rhythm, rhyme, images; events, dates, places; and the like. Let's return to Ralph, who has yet another paper to write for his course on Victorian England. Now he's analyzing the novel *Jane Eyre*, so he created the following analysis frame:

Jane Eyre

Main Characters	Settings	Plot
Jane Eyre (plucky governess, heroine) Mr. Rochester (love interest, mysterious master of Thornfield) Adele (cute little girl whom Jane teaches; Mr. R. is her guardian) Aunt Reed (cruel woman who takes care of Jane as child)	Thornfield—Mr. Rochester's estate Lowood—horrible school where Jane is sent by evil Aunt Reed Aunt Reed's house—name? (*Go back and check!*)	Jane is a misunderstood child. Badly treated by Aunt Reed, sent to a horrible school, although later the school gets better. (*How much time to take with this?*) The good part: Jane, grown up, goes to Thornfield, where she falls in love with Mr. R. But can the rich man love a poor governess? He pro-poses marriage to her, but it turns out he has a horrible secret . . . .

As you can see, Ralph uses his graphic organizer to get his thoughts together. He comments on points that he wants to think about more, notes his questions about what to do next, uses abbreviations and slang—in short, he does whatever helps him identify important ideas.

Of course the headings for an analysis frame won't always be "Main Characters," "Settings," and "Plot." If Ruth were using an analysis frame for her paper on U.S.-Japanese relations, her headings might be "Times When Relations Were Good," "Times When Relations Were Bad," "Reasons Relations Improved," and "Reasons Relations Got Worse." Deciding what the categories are for your analysis frame is part of thinking through the topic.

MAKE A PRO-CON CHART

A *pro-con chart* can help you with the following kinds of writing:

- Problem-and-solution essay
- Editorial
- Persuasive essay
- Business letter
- Memo

Basically, a pro-con chart helps you explore both the positive and the negative aspects of an idea. As you might imagine, this is a useful thing to do even if—especially if—you already have a strong opinion on a topic.

Let's say, for example, that Jocelyn, the personnel manager who had to write a memo on reducing employee turnover, decided to focus her memo on offering flex-time, a kind of flexible scheduling that allows employees to work a fixed number of hours, but not necessarily from 9:00 to 5:00. Naturally, her memo will list *pro* arguments: "Flex-time has been shown to boost employee productivity." But to be really effective, it should also respond to the *con* arguments, or objections, her opponents might present.

Jocelyn anticipates those objections and thinks of ways to answer them: "Some may argue that flex-time presents communication problems, since not everyone is in the office at the same time. This problem can be easily overcome in the following ways . . . ."

A pro-and-con chart is a good way to graphically present pro and con arguments.

Flex-Time	
Pros	**Cons**
Some people work better at different times of day	Communication problems—not everyone in office at same time
Good for parents	
	Employees harder to supervise
People produce better work when relaxed	

If you wanted, you could make little notes after the pros, the cons, or both. For example, if you're making the chart so that you can write a memo supporting flex-time, you might want to note possible solutions after each con item. Or you might revise the chart to include a column headed "Solutions." Also remember: You don't have to mention every pro or con in your actual memo, especially if you've been asked to write a brief memo. But making this chart ensures that you know what all the arguments are, so that you can choose the ones that best fit your writing purpose and your audience.

MAKE A COMPARISON-AND-CONTRAST CHART

If you have to write a *comparison-and-contrast essay,* this is the graphic organizer for you. It is also useful for writing a:

- Comparative analysis of two products
- Proposal
- Letter to the editor

The goal of this type of chart is to help you identify similarities and differences. Jocelyn, our friendly personnel director grappling with the problem of employee turnover, compares and contrasts two insurance companies, one with high turnover and one with low.

<table>
<tr><td align="center">Roadrunner
Insurance Company
(low turnover)</td><td align="center">Coyote
Insurance Company
(high turnover)</td></tr>
</table>

── Similarities ──

Workforce Size:
Both have about 500 workers

Location:
Both are located in Metropolis, a large metropolitan area

Type of Work:
Both are insurance companies

Benefits:
Similar medical coverage
Both offer partial reimbursement for college course

── Differences ──

Vacation Policy:

Offers 2 weeks vacation after four years	Offers 4 weeks vacation after four years

Work Hours:

8-hour days on flex-time	Strict 9-to-5 hours for all

Jocelyn's chart brings out a pretty strong point for her memo. The two insurance companies are similar in almost every way. But even though Coyote offers longer vacations, they have higher turnover than Road Runner. What's the only other difference? Road Runner offers flex-time!

MAKE A VENN DIAGRAM

Another way to compare and contrast two things is by making a *Venn diagram:* two overlapping circles. The part where the circles overlap shows what the two items have in common. The part where each circle is separate shows how each item is unique.

Here's how Joshua might use a Venn diagram to compare and contrast "Home Work" with an "Office Work" schedule:

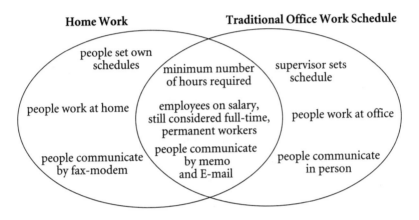

Home Work   **Traditional Office Work Schedule**

people set own schedules

people work at home

people communicate by fax-modem

minimum number of hours required

employees on salary, still considered full-time, permanent workers

people communicate by memo and E-mail

supervisor sets schedule

people work at office

people communicate in person

Now Joshua can see clearly where the two schedules are different and where they intersect. This gives a clear pictorial representation of the situation.

MAKE A FLOW CHART

A *flow chart* outlines the steps in a process. You can use it to help you prepare the following types of writing:

- Process analysis (a fancy way to say "explanation of how something works")
- Cause-and-effect essay
- How-to essay
- Research report
- Proposal
- Technical description

The effectiveness of the flow chart is that it clearly shows the steps or stages in a process. Here is the flow chart Maria prepared to report on the results of a science experiment:

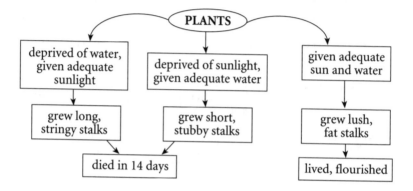

By putting her thoughts into the form of a flow chart, Maria has formed a clear idea of how each step in the experiment led to a particular result. This clarity will make it easier for her to write an effective report.

MAKE A PROBLEM-AND-SOLUTION CHART

As the name suggests, this type of chart helps you explore a problem and its possible solutions. Use it to help you write an editorial, as well as a:

- Problem-and-solution essay
- Persuasive essay
- Business letter
- Proposal
- Memo

Suppose you are on a parents' committee to improve the schools in your neighborhood. You have taken on the job of writing a proposal dealing with the problem of overcrowding in the elementary school.

Problem:	Goal:
Oakdale Elementary School is too crowded. Too many kids in each classroom. Not enough books to go around.	To alleviate overcrowding at the Oakdale Elementary School.
Possible Solutions:	**Pros (+) and Cons (−):**
Build an addition on to the school and hire more teachers.	+ Fewer children in each class. More room. − Too expensive. Would raise taxes.
Transfer some children to neighboring districts where enrollment is lower.	+ Fewer children in the school. − Many parents would object. They moved to this district because of the excellent schools. Also, too much emotional upheaval for children.
Have kids start middle school at grade 5 instead of grade 6. There's more room in the middle school.	+ Fewer children in elementary school. − Some kids may be too emotionally immature to deal with middle-school atmosphere.
Preferred Solution:	**Reason(s):**
Send grade 5 to the middle school.	Solves problem with least expense and upheaval.

In this systematic way, the parent's committee could find the solution that will satisfy the most people. It is made clear by using such a diagrammatic representation.

FELICIA ORGANIZES HER IDEAS

We find our heroine, Felicia, mulling over her ideas. She has actually decided that the best way to organize her ideas would be by using an *analysis frame*. This is the only graphic organizer she feels would work for her from the ones we've discussed. She is not weighing pros and cons, she is not comparing or contrasting ideas, she is not explaining a process, and she is not solving a problem. So she is left with the analysis frame. Here is what it might look like:

What I've Learned from Studying T'ai Chi

What I Expected from T'ai Chi	Why I Wanted to Quit
Expected it to come easy—used to doing well without working too hard	Wasn't doing well, even when I worked hard
Expected to excel—used to being best in class	Teacher embarrassed me in front of class

What Made Me Keep Going	How I Gained Emotional Strength
Teacher explained that someone will always be better	Now I am able to keep trying even when I think I might not succeed
Teacher made me see being the best—or even succeeding—is not always the best motive for doing something	A good lesson for life

Plug In

Will any of the graphic organizers help you think further about the topic you've chosen? If so, use one or more of them to develop your ideas. If not, but you feel like practicing, choose one of the following writing tasks.

- Use an analysis frame to start a response to a book, poem, or play.

- Make a pro-con chart about a topic that will be the subject of an office memo.

- Create a comparison-and-contrast chart to compare two proposed solutions to a problem at your school or workplace.

- Make a Venn diagram to compare two historical figures or two (real or imaginary) candidates for public office.

- Make a flow chart to show how to do something, such as prepare a recipe or complete a simple home repair.

- Make a problem-and-solution chart to help you prepare a memo proposing some change at your office or school.

CHAPTER TEN

Putting Your Ideas in Order

You're getting there. You've got your ideas pretty well firmed up. Your job now is to decide in what order to present them. After you have figured this out, you can make an outline and then you will be just about home free. And, actually, once you have got that outline, your piece of writing "writes itself."

But for now, let's stick to the task at hand: getting your ideas in the best

order possible. As you consider your options, you will see that the order in which you present your ideas has a lot to do with your writing purpose and with your audience. Remember them?

CHRONOLOGICAL ORDER

If your writing purpose is to tell a story, write about your life, describe an historical event, or summarize the plot of a book or movie, you will probably want to use *chronological order*. This is the order in which things actually happened.

Here's how Malcolm began to list the events in his story about Roberto Suarez:

1. 7th grade. I didn't know Roberto well. Tell my impressions of him.
2. One day, social studies teacher—Mr. Ford—assigned term paper on a European country, our choice.
3. Roberto said, "Why always Europe? Why not Latin America?"
4. I expected teacher to get mad. But he said, "Okay, Latin Am., your choice."
5. Students surprised. Roberto had always been quiet. Now he was questioning a teacher's assignment. And the teacher wasn't even mad.
6. Term papers turned in.
7. Term papers back. R. gets an A!!! Teacher explains: Part of learning is taking an active part in your own education.
8. What I learned from that is . . .

ORDER OF IMPORTANCE

Order of importance is useful for the purpose of building an argument, writing a news story, outlining a proposal, or analyzing a topic in literature or history. Order of importance can work two ways:

1. Start with the *least* important idea and build up to the *most* important. This is known as *ascending* order of importance.
2. Start with the *most* important idea and work down to the *least* important. This is known as *descending* order of importance.

Let's go back to Jocelyn's memo about flex-time on the job. She has already prepared a pro-con chart and made a comparison-and-contrast chart to organize her ideas. Now she is ready to put her ideas in order. She is going to use *ascending* order of importance, which is the way we most often argue and describe incidents in real life. For example: "Guess who was there? The mayor, the governor, and—the president!" It would sound wrong to start with the president and end with the mayor. But back to Jocelyn and her flex-time writing task:

Why We Need Flex-Time

Point 1:   People more comfortable working on individualized schedules.

(Give personal example; cite employee survey.)

Point 2:   Parents, especially, could benefit from flex-time. *(Give example of how parents could use flex-time. Maybe quote from parent who wants it?)*

Point 3:   True, there are arguments against flex-time: communication problems—not everyone in office at same time; employees harder to supervise. Can be solved: have weekly meetings, have employees submit weekly progress reports to supervisors.

Point 4:   The bottom line is that flex-time improves productivity: allows more individual freedom, so people accomplish more.

Point 5:   Cite statistics showing how productivity goes up. Compare and contrast Coyote Insurance Company with Road Runner.

Notice how Jocelyn saved for *last* the argument that will make the *strongest* impression on her audience, who happens to be her boss.

For an example of *descending* order of importance, take a look at any news story in your daily paper. The *lead*, or first paragraph, tells you the most important thing about the story. That's supposed to grab your interest and get you to read further. The reporter follows with the next most important fact, then the next, and so on. That way, if you (the audience) stop reading at any point, you have still learned the most important information.

You might also use descending order of importance if you are writing a letter or memo to someone whom you suspect will not read it very carefully. Here is how you might put your ideas in *descending* order of importance for a letter to our old friend Mr. Skeffington, the guy from *Iguana Monthly:*

1. Stop billing me!

2. Tell credit bureaus I'm not delinquent.

3. I never ordered this magazine.

4. I know you're busy, life is tough, mistakes get made.

With this order, even if Mr. Skeffington is too bored or too busy to read the whole letter, he will at least have understood the main purpose of your letter: to get him to stop billing you. He can hand the letter to a subordinate, call the billing department, or take whatever action is necessary, even if he doesn't finish reading the letter.

The same principle can apply to a letter to a prospective employer. Again, your audience is a busy person who will want you to get right to the point:

1. I have had three years of experience in this field.

2. I have had four years of experience in related fields.

3. I have a degree from business school.

4. I learn fast and I am fun to work with.

Your hope is that the first item impresses the employer enough to cause him or her to read the second; the second entices him or her on to read the third; and so on. If the employer has to wait until the end of the letter to find that you have three years of experience in the field, you may have lost his or her attention.

ORDER OF IMPRESSION

If your writing purpose is to describe a person, place, or experience, you might use *order of impression*. Start with the first thing you noticed, continue on to the next, and so on. Margarita used this order for part of her essay about her Grandma Rose:

1. First thing you notice: This is a stubborn old lady!

2. Then she offers you food: She's generous!

3. Talk with her a while, you find she puts family first, always.

4. When I learned about her background, I found out she was brave.

5. Here's an old photograph I once saw. Sexy smile!

6. I found out more about her background . . . 13 kids! Three died . . .

By using this order, Margarita gives readers the feeling that they, too, are getting to know Grandma Rose. She starts with the first thing she thinks her audience would notice about her grandmother and moves on to all the other things we might notice or find out.

SPATIAL ORDER

If you are describing a building, a work of art, or a natural scene, you might use *spatial order* as an alternative to order of impression. You could start with the nearest item and work your way to the item farthest away; or you might start with the farthest and work your way up to the nearest. You could go from right to left or vice versa; or from top to bottom or vice versa. Here is an example:

1. Heavy old door, opens into darkness

2. Switch on the light; dusty, musty

3. Red plush seats, worn, patches showing through

4. Huge stage, stretches back into darkness

5. Look up to ceiling─ornate gold cupids and flowering vines

The reader feels as though he or she has just walked into the old, unused theater. Your description of the spatial order has led the reader along carefully.

FELICIA GETS HER IDEAS IN ORDER

As we join her, we notice that Felicia has run into a problem. You may very well run into the same one. It is not clear to her what kind of order she should use. Ascending order of importance makes sense to her. Chronological order seems like a good idea too. After all, she wants to tell the story of her experiences with t'ai chi as well as get across an idea.

The good news for Felicia, and for you too, is that it is perfectly acceptable—and usually quite necessary—to *combine different types or order*. So Felicia can start with chronological order, telling about her experiences in the order in which they happened. Then she can switch over to ascending order of importance. Here's how she did it:

1. Started t'ai chi expecting to learn easily and be best in class.
2. It didn't turn out that way. Felt awkward and clumsy. Others better than I was.
3. One day teacher embarrassed me in class by criticizing my form.
4. I kept practicing, even though I wanted to give up.
5. Teacher said, "Not so bad. Now work more!"
6. Teacher made a speech. Said that someone would always be better, no matter how good you are. Being the best is not the reason for trying.
7. I realized he was talking about me.

Up to point 7, Felicia's order has been chronological. Now notice what she does.

8. I learned three important things:
   - The most important things don't always come easy.
   - You don't have to always be the best.
   - Most important: You must keep trying, even when you think you might fail.

Plug In

Now it's your turn to pick up where you left off organizing your ideas and actually put those ideas in order. Here's what we'd like you to do.

First: Decide on the type of order that will be most appropriate for your topic.

Then: Make a numbered list.

Then: By all means, combine two or more types of order, if necessary.

Hey—whatever works!

CHAPTER ELEVEN

Making a Formal Outline

This is it—your last step before getting down to writing this thing of yours! As we mentioned, this is where it all comes together, so that when you do write, it goes more smoothly than you could possibly imagine. This is what all this prewriting stuff has been leading up to.

POWER LINE

But even the kind of writing that is essentially adventurous and impetuous will on examination be found to have a secret plan: Columbus didn't just sail, he sailed west, and the New World took shape from this simple and, we now think, sensible design.

—E. B. White, *Elements of Style*

THE THREE-LEVEL FORMAL OUTLINE

You have seen formal outlines. They have topics that begin with Roman numerals (I, II, III, etcetera), with capital letters, with Arabic numerals, and sometimes with lowercase letters. We are going to stick to a three-level formal outline—the kind that has Roman numerals, capital letters, and Arabic numerals as headings. The best way to understand a formal outline is to look at an example. Explaining just makes it all sound too confusing—and it is not. Here is the outline Malcolm made from his chronological list of ideas for his essay about Roberto Suarez.

Title: "Roberto Suarez: Someone Who Influenced Me"

Thesis Statement: Because he questioned a decision made by an authority figure, Robert Suarez influenced me by teaching me to stand up for what I believe in.

I. Background

    A. What we learned in social studies
        1. Studied history
        2. Learned to write term papers

    B. Mr. Ford (teacher)
        1. Tough, but fair
        2. Insisted on discipline
        3. Assigned term paper on a European country

    C. Roberto Suarez
        1. Quiet and reserved
        2. Not an outstanding student
        3. Seemed lonely and angry

II. The incident

    A. Roberto's reaction to the assignment
        1. Challenged Mr. Ford
        2. Wanted to write about a Latin American country

    B. Mr. Ford's reaction to Roberto
        1. Gave Roberto permission
        2. Didn't get angry

    C. Class's reaction
        1. Everyone surprised at Roberto
        2. Everyone surprised at Mr. Ford

III. What happened to Roberto

    A. Got A on paper

    B. Was happy

    C. Won respect of the class

IV. What I learned

    A. That people can surprise you

    B. That you should stand up for what you believe in

Notice two key features of Malcolm's outline:

- Each lower-level idea directly supports the higher-level idea above it.
- There are always at least two ideas at each level

You will never see a "1." without at least a "2." following it under the same capital letter. Likewise, you will never find an "A." without at least a "B." under the same Roman numeral.

FELICIA MAKES AN OUTLINE

Here is one more example: Felicia's outline for her college-application essay about what she learned from t'ai chi. It looks like the essay is shaping up pretty well!

Title: "What I Learned from Studying T'ai Chi"

Thesis Statement: T'ai chi has taught me to keep trying, even if I think I might fail.

I. What I expected from t'ai chi

    A. Started out expecting to learn easily

        1. Used to learning easily

        2. Had lots of self-confidence

    B. Expected to be best in class

        1. Usually best in class

        2. Thought it was important to be best

 111

      C. Expected praise from teacher
          1. Praised by other teachers
          2. Thought praise was important

II. How my experience was different from my expectations

      A. Difficult to learn
          1. Felt awkward and clumsy
          2. Wasn't best–others better

      B. Criticized by teacher–not praised
          1. Felt embarrassed
          2. Wanted to give up

III. How I responded to experience

      A. Kept practicing
      B. Refused to give up, even when teacher said, "Not so bad. Now work more!"
      C. Knew teacher was talking about me when he gave speech

IV. What I learned

      A. Praise is not the most important thing
      B. The most rewarding things don't always come easy
      C. You don't have to always be the best
      D. Most important: Keep trying, even when you think you might fail

Plug In

Take the final step of prewriting: Look back at the work you have done on your two-page essay or your five-minute speech. On a separate sheet of paper, organize your thoughts into a three-level formal outline that will help you write on the topic you've chosen.

Then turn to the next section to learn about first drafts—at long last.

SECTION THREE

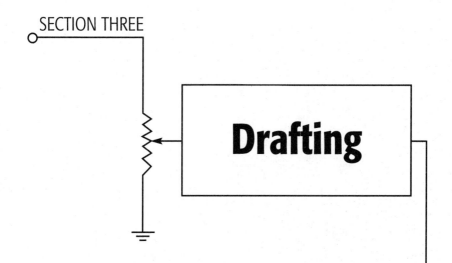

Drafting

Jump In and Write

This is where you get to dig in and get to work. Look over this section. By the time you have done all the work of getting ready to write (prewriting), this part, the drafting part, will go much more smoothly than you think. The main thing is to just jump in and write.

Warming Up. Go back and look at your notes, exercises, and outlines. Memorize your thesis statement, or paste it somewhere nearby so you can glance up and see it now and then. Make sure you have everything you need near your desk or table, the ringer on the phone is turned off, and you have a stretch of free time of at least two hours.

Stretching. Use a combination of prewriting techniques and drafting as described in the following section. Play music if that helps. Take this part seriously. By that, we mean allow for this time for yourself. This work is important for many reasons.

Working Out. After you have roughed out the draft, work on the beginning. This is what will make the biggest impression on your reader. Either they will keep going or put your paper or memo to the side. Try a quotation, a scene, some startling statistics. You are now firing up your reader to care about what you are going to tell him or her.

Training. Use examples, details, descriptions, quotes, and statistics, and make the draft mean something. Keep the reader reading. Take some time for this, letting your imagination enter here: What would really be a grabber? What would make the reader remember this paper? What makes this something you want to read about?

Sprint. Set aside time for this every day when your deadline is getting closer. Even if you do not want to do it, sit at your desk and begin. Make a note or two to yourself at the end of each session about where you need to pick up on the next day. This will help on those mornings when even a second cup of coffee does not get you going. Your note will tell you: Start here. Do not pass go . . . you know the routine.

Marathon. When things are going well, keep at it. If you can call a friend and cancel lunch because you are moving along so well, do that. Your friend will understand and you will have that much more time the next day.

Cooling Down. Relax. Let your first draft sit for a few days if possible. Go see a movie. Come back to it for the revision stage fresh.

Personal Best. Pretend you are just seeing your draft for the first time when you come back to it, refreshed and relaxed. You are ready to revise!

READY TO DRAFT

> **POWER LINE**
>
> I start at the beginning, go on to the end, and then stop.
>
> –Anthony Burgess

You've thought (and thought and thought) about your writing project. So enough thinking and prewriting already. It's time to act. If you've followed all of the steps of Section Two, you now have, right in your hot little hand, a formal outline of what you intend to write. It's got Roman numerals, capital letters, Arabic numerals, and possibly even lowercase letters, and it's ready—even begging!—to be turned into a genuine, bona fide piece of writing.

CHAPTER TWELVE

Writing the Draft

What's the difference between drafting and writing?

Engrave this answer on your heart. If necessary, copy it in bright red ink and post it over your desk: "A draft is not final. You can always change it!" You might get more ideas as you write. You might change your mind about your thesis or your supporting ideas. (We hope you won't change your mind about your topic itself, but anything's possible.) You will almost certainly see better ways to use words and sentences and better ways to organize your writing. And it would be downright weird if you didn't need to fix some spelling and punctuation errors. If you think of your first draft as final in any sense, you're liable to freeze up, which makes writing much harder than it needs to be. The best way to prevent those "Blank Pages Blues" is to keep repeating, "It's only a draft . . . ."

PLAN AHEAD

Make sure you have everything you need. Here's a checklist of some resources that might be helpful to have within arm's reach of your work area, so you don't have to get up and look for them when you need them. Of course, if you're riding the wave of that writing energy and you're too impatient to look at this list, by all means, don't let us stop you! Plunge right in. You can always come back to this later. For those of you willing to postpone the moment of truth for a few more minutes, however, read on.

Equip Your Work Area. Here are some things you might need:

- Samples of similar types of writing. If you're writing a memo, for example, you might want copies of some other successful office memos, so you can follow in the footsteps of other writers.
- A copy of the application or guidelines if you're writing an essay for a college, graduate school, internship, fellowship, or grant program.
- Adequate writing supplies—pen, pencil, paper, printer cartridges, whatever you need. If you are using a computer, you might actually want those outmoded items—paper and a pen—handy for jotting down quick notes.
- Something soothing (and nonalcoholic) to drink, so you don't have to keep getting up.

Of course, it goes without saying that you're working in a well-lit, comfortable space that is either quiet or flavored with some nondistracting music. Work in a space that is free of interruptions and distractions. If possible, put on the answering machine or let voicemail pick up the telephone.

WAYS OF DRAFTING

There are actually several ways to draft. Here are three we know of. Perhaps you'll discover some others.

1. Write a Quick Loose Draft

Perhaps you have carefully followed the prewriting suggestions in the earlier chapters. Or maybe you haven't. Maybe you haven't got any prewriting plans at all, and don't have time to make them. Okay. Don't panic. Just start. Seriously, just start.

POWER LINE

My schedule is flexible but I am rather particular about my instruments; lined Bristol cards and well sharpened, not too hard pencils capped with erasers.

—Vladimir Nabokov

Pick up a pen or put your hands on a keyboard, and write down the first thing about your topic that you can think of. Here are some guidelines for this drafting method.

- Keep going. No, don't stop and tell yourself how stupid this is. You can do that later if it's really absolutely necessary.

- Don't worry about using complete sentences or finding exactly the right word.

- If you know something is needed and you can't think of the words, leave yourself a note: "More about Uncle Bert here" or "Tell Massapequa story."

- When you've finished, take a break. A big break, like overnight. (Unless, of course, it's midnight and your deadline is tomorrow. In that case, take a very tiny break, drink some coffee, and forge ahead—with our sympathies.)

- Come back to your work refreshed (or not, as the case may be), colored pencil in hand. Slowly, breathing deeply, read over your work.

- Cross out the stuff you don't want, and reorganize and elaborate on the stuff you do want. Fill in those blank spaces until you've got something worthy of being called a rough draft. Then you'll be ready to revise and repair.

2. Write a Slow, Tight Draft

> **POWER LINE**
>
> The best regimen is to get up early, insult yourself a bit in the shaving mirror, and then pretend you're cutting wood.
>
> –Lawrence Durrell

Suppose you have a good working outline. Or suppose that you have a really clear, logical mind, and ideas just naturally present themselves to you in a useable order. We have only met one or two writers like this in our lifetime, but they do exist. If you are one, congratulations! You've won the writing lottery. In either case, you'll prepare a draft one paragraph at a time, supporting each of your main ideas with details. If you're using a formal outline, each capital letter might correspond to a paragraph's main idea, with the Arabic numerals (1, 2, 3, and so on) corresponding to the details. This method will probably produce a fairly readable draft that bears a strong resemblance to your final product. However, even this type of draft is likely to require revisions. But don't worry about that now.

3. Write a Combination Draft

Perhaps most of your draft will be well-organized, following your outline. But every so often, you might sketch in something. Perhaps your prewriting will help you structure most of your essay, but you will write a loose introduction and conclusion. Perhaps you will write a well-organized draft all the way through, but keep making notes to yourself about things you'd like to add or change. This is a fine way to proceed: it combines logic and freedom.

USE PREWRITING TECHNIQUES AS YOU DRAFT

You may breeze through some parts of your draft and feel completely stuck in others. That's okay. Just pick your favorite prewriting technique, such as freewriting or brainstorming, to get yourself going again.

Although we've broken writing into three stages—prewriting, drafting, and revising—in real life, writers move back and forth among these stages. For example, if you were cleaning up a huge, dirty kitchen, you might first clear the table and all the counters (prewriting), then wash all dirty dishes (writing), then wipe off the counters and sweep the floor (revising). But you also might clear some dishes, wash some of them but leave the pans to soak, straighten up a bit, clear some more dishes, and so on.

Whether you're cleaning a kitchen or writing an essay, we advise you to develop the process that works best for you.

> ○⌇⌇∿ **POWER LINE** ∿⌇⌇○
>
> I'll write a very rough first draft of every chapter, then I will rewrite every chapter. I try to get it down in the first rewrite, but some chapters I can't quite get right the third time. There are some I go over and over and over again.
>
> –Robert Stone

A WORD ABOUT THE SAMPLES

One of the best ways of learning to write is by example. So throughout the chapters in Section Three, we'll be giving you lots of writing samples to look at. We had a hard decision to make with this section—whether to provide real first-draft samples in all their roughness, or to give you samples that were in pretty good shape. We decided on the latter. That way you can actually use the samples to help with your own writing.

CHAPTER THIRTEEN

Writing a Good Beginning

We keep promising that now is when you get to start writing, but then we keep jabbering on about it. Okay—now we really mean it. You're about to write your first paragraph. In that paragraph, you'll want to accomplish two important goals:

1. Grab the interest of your readers.

2. Give them a preview of what they're about to read.

> ⌇**POWER LINE**⌇
>
> With me, a story usually begins with a single idea or memory or mental picture. The writing of the story is simply a matter of working up to that moment, to explain why it happened or what caused it to follow.
>
> —William Faulkner

When a movie begins and while the credits are on the screen, you get curious and want to keep watching. That is what a beginning paragraph should do for a piece of writing: It makes you want to sit there and see what will happen next. Here are several approaches you could take at the beginning of your opus.

STATE YOUR MAIN IDEA

Remember Jocelyn, back in the personnel department? She's finally ready to write her memo summarizing her findings on how to reduce employee turnover. Straightforward type that she is, she decides to start with her main idea, which is basically her thesis statement, slightly "souped up":

The average employee in our company works here about eight months. The ideal average is at least two years. To bring us closer to that ideal, I'm proposing a flex-time program that allows employees to decide on the schedules that best fit into their individual lives. Surveys and statistics show that companies offering more flexible work schedules have lower employee turnover.

Jocelyn gets her readers' attention by zooming in on her company's problem. Then she comes right in with a way to solve it. Next, Jocelyn will go on to define flex-time, explain its benefits and anticipate and answer possible arguments against it. Finally, she will make her most important point: Flex-time improves productivity as well as reducing employee turnover. She can cite her comparison and contrast between Road Runner and Coyote Insurance companies to support her claim. See what we mean by a piece of cake?

ASK A QUESTION

Joshua, our other personnel director, is writing a memo on improving employee morale by allowing employees to work at home a certain number of hours each week. He begins his memo with a question. Starting out this way gets readers thinking about his topic right from the start, because most of us, when asked a question, have an instant reaction: We try to answer it. Here's how Joshua starts his memo:

What's the biggest problem facing our company? Employee morale. And low morale means low productivity. Since many of our employees are parents with heavy responsibilities at home as well as at work, having the option of working at home a certain number of hours each week would be sure to raise their morale. It would raise their productivity as well.

See how Joshua prepares readers for what he is about to tell them?

START WITH A GREAT FACT OR STATISTIC

Let's say you are still working on that proposal to solve the overcrowding problem in your kids' elementary school. How about this, for a starter?

> Fact: Children who come from elementary school classes of fewer than 25 students average 20 points higher on standardized tests than those who come from classrooms of 26 or more. At the Oakdale Elementary School, the average class size is 35 students. While there are many valid reasons for reducing class size, this fact alone should be enough to convince parents in this community that something must be done. Of the three possible solutions, the one that costs the least money and makes the most sense is moving the fifth grade to the middle school, where there is plenty of room.

Bet you'll get parents' attention with that one! Scare tactics work great—especially when you back them up with statistics.

CITE A QUOTATION

Clever quotations by famous people or even not-so-famous people are another way to get your readers to sit up and take notice. Quotations are particularly effective in beginning personal and persuasive essays. Here's a quote we could have used for this book:

> "There's nothing to writing," the renowned sportswriter, Red Smith, once said. "All you do is sit down and open a vein." True, many writers find writing difficult. But we're going to introduce you to four golden rules that will make your task much simpler.

For another example, here's how Margarita started her personal essay about her grandmother:

> "Remember, cara mia, you must always be true to your dream!" I can still see my Grandma Rose smiling as she says this, her sharp eyes gazing intently into mine. It is because of what Grandma Rose taught me that I was able to realize my dream of becoming a dancer.

FELICIA TELLS AN ANECDOTE

Everyone loves a story. Our friend Felicia chose to start the first draft for her college-application essay about t'ai chi by telling a short story or anecdote that makes her point.

> Once a master jeweler had an impatient pupil. The day of the first lesson, the Master handed his pupil a piece of jade and shut him in a room. When two hours had passed, he released the boy without a word. The day of the second lesson, the same thing happened. This continued for several months, until finally the pupil said, "Now, look, Master. I wanted to study with you, and I've done everything you said. But you've taught me nothing. You've just handed me a piece of jade and locked me in a room every day. And today you gave me a fake piece of jade!" The Master answered, "If you've learned nothing, how did you know the jade was fake?"
>
> In my t'ai chi class, I was much like the pupil in the story. I didn't think I was making progress. Then, just as I was getting impatient and ready to give up, I found that there was hope for me after all.

An anecdote makes a particularly good beginning for a personal essay like Felicia's—also for a speech or a persuasive essay.

Plug In

Which type of introduction will work best for your essay or speech? Keeping in mind your purpose and your audience, experiment with one or two versions of your introduction. Remember, just do it! You can (and will) revise later. Try any of the ideas we have suggested:

- State your main idea
- Ask a question
- Start with an interesting fact or statistic
- Cite a quotation
- Tell an anecdote

CHAPTER FOURTEEN

Writing the Main Body

Now it is time to write the main part of your essay, speech, or report. In your first paragraph, you've prepared readers for the key ideas you plan to present. In the main part of your writing, you will elaborate on these ideas, or tell more about them, by providing details. "What kinds of details?" you may be asking. Here are some ideas.

> ◦ᴧᴧᴧᴠ◦ **POWER LINE** ◦ᴧᴧᴧᴠ◦
>
> All writing is ultimately a question of solving a problem. It may be a problem of where to obtain facts, or how to organize the material. It may be a problem of approach or attitude, tone, or style. Whatever it is, it has to be confronted and solved.
>
> –William Zinsser, *On Writing Well*

USE FACTS AND STATISTICS

Especially when you are trying to persuade readers to agree with a point you are making, you need hard facts to back up your opinion. If the facts include numbers, so much the better. There's nothing like numbers to convince readers that you know what you're talking about.

Here, for example, is a paragraph from the end of Jocelyn's memo on "Why We Need Flex-Time." Notice how Jocelyn uses facts and statistics to lend authority to her writing:

> Finally, an analysis of employee turnover at two major insurance companies, Road Runner and Coyote, demonstrates that the turnover at Road Runner—the company that offers employees a flex-time option—is 30 percent lower. The two insurance companies are similar in the

following ways: both have approximately 500 employees, both are located in a large metropolitan area, and both offer a similar benefits package, including medical and dental coverage plus partial reimbursement for college courses. Even though Coyote offers four weeks of vacation after four years, while Road Runner offers only two, Road Runner still maintains a much higher rate of employee satisfaction, resulting in a much lower rate of turnover.

USE EXAMPLES

Which of the following statements do you find more convincing?

There are many advantages to living in an urban area. Give me the city any day! I'd go crazy living in the suburbs.

There are many advantages to living in a city; for example, city dwellers have easier access to public transportation, cultural events, and social gatherings.

The second sentence is more convincing because the writer provides concrete examples to back up her opinion, whereas the writer of the first sentence just keeps repeating his own opinion, using different words.

Here is a way you might use examples to prove your point that the Oakdale Elementary School is too crowded:

It is clear that the Oakdale School is overcrowded. For example, we do not have enough books to go around; in some rooms, children have to share desks; and with so many students in each class, it is impossible for teachers to give each student the individual attention she or he needs.

Using the phrase "For example . . . " to introduce your examples lets the reader know what to expect next—but it's not always necessary.

USE DEFINITIONS AND EXPLANATIONS

If you are using terms or concepts with which your readers may be unfamiliar, you'll need to explain them. For example, Maria, the student who was writing a lab report about her science experiment with plants, should clearly define any technical terms she uses. The terms defined are in italics. Notice the three different ways Maria defines terms to make her writing understandable:

> Whether they are *herbivores* (plant-eaters) or *carnivores* (meat-eaters), animals depend on *locomotion*, or the ability to move from one place to another, to find food. Because plants, unlike animals, do not have locomotion, they have to make their own food. The process by which green plants manufacture their own food is called *photosynthesis*, and to complete this process, plants need three things: sunlight, air, and water.

Maria enclosed her definitions for herbivores and carnivores in parentheses; she used the word *or* to define the term locomotion; and she used the phrase *is called* to define photosynthesis.

USE SENSORY DETAILS

Images that evoke sight, sound, smell, taste, and touch make descriptive writing more concrete and vivid. The more precise your details, the more your readers will feel like they can actually experience the person, place, or object you are describing. This kind of elaboration is especially useful in personal essays and news writing.

ᴘᴏᴡᴇʀ ʟɪɴᴇ ᴏᴡᴍᴡᴏ

If those who have studied the art of writing are in accord on any one point, it is on this: the surest way to arouse and hold the attention of the reader is by being specific, definite, and concrete. Homer, Dante, Shakespeare are effective largely because they deal in particulars and report the details that matter. Their words call up pictures.

—E. B. White, *Elements of Style*

Margarita jotted down a list of sensory images that evoked her grandmother:

Sight:	sharp eyes, pink rosebuds embroidered on apron
Sound:	her laugh goes from high note to low
Smell:	her lavender perfume

Taste:	garlic in everything she cooks
Touch:	soft, wrinkled cheek; rough skin on her fingers

Then Margarita used some of these images to make her essay more vivid:

> My grandmother puts her arms around me and holds me close. I feel her velvety, wrinkled cheek next to mine and smell the sweet scent of her lavender perfume. I am amazed that this old woman, so soft and gentle, has survived a lifetime of adventure, joy, and tragedy.

FELICIA USES PERSONAL FEELINGS, MEMORIES, AND ANECDOTES

Including these in your writing can add interest, emotional depth, humor, and even credibility to your work. Use them freely in a personal essay or memoir, but for any kind of business or formal writing, use them very sparingly. Notice how Felicia effectively expresses personal feelings in this part of a paragraph from the main body of her essay:

> Looking back, I can't believe how confidently I walked into class for my first t'ai chi lesson. Used to learning new things quickly and easily, I was sure that by my third or fourth lesson I'd be the best student in the class. In fact, not only did I expect to be the best, I expected to be recognized as the best by my fellow students as well as by my teacher. But it didn't turn out exactly that way.

Plug In

Decide on the one or more kinds of details you will add to the ideas you focused on in prewriting.

- Is your purpose to prove a point?
- Do you use facts, statistics, and examples to back up your opinions?
- Is your purpose to describe a place so vividly your readers will feel that they've been there?

- Do you use precise details that appeal to as many of the five senses as possible?
- Is your purpose to give information? If so, do you clearly define and explain your terms?

Now, write a first draft of the main part of the essay or speech you've been working on. If you like, take your time and write a slow tight draft that's as close to perfect as you can make it. That means you'll be changing lots of words and sentences as you go along.

If you think you'd prefer to just get it all down any way it comes out and then fix it later, then write a quick loose draft.

Either way, don't forget—first (as in "first draft") means first, not last, not final, not etched in stone, not set in concrete. One other thing to remember: When you finish the main part of your writing, your writing isn't finished. You still get to wrap it all up with a really smashing conclusion.

CHAPTER FIFTEEN

Writing a Strong Conclusion

The conclusion is your last chance to make your point. So you want to be sure that your concluding paragraph serves your purpose and reaches your audience. Whatever you say at the end is what readers will remember.

⌇⌇⌇ **POWER LINE** ⌇⌇⌇

The perfect ending should take the reader slightly by surprise and yet seem exactly right to him.

–William Zinsser, *On Writing Well*

ALL'S WELL THAT ENDS WELL

A good conclusion might do any or all of the following things:

Summarize for your reader. This method has the advantage of leaving your readers with a clear, concise version of your main points.

Restate your main idea. If you have won readers over with your forceful arguments, persuasive reasons, and illuminating examples, you can now drive home your point by repeating your main idea. Just think how good it will sound now that they are ready to agree with you!

Leave the reader with a strong impression. Whether it's a general impression or a visual image to remember, be sure your writing will keep coming back to "haunt" the reader well after he or she has finished reading.

Recommend a course of action. What should readers think or do if they agree with you? Tell them, in no uncertain terms.

Bring your main idea to life. Tell an anecdote, quote someone famous (or not famous), ask a thought-provoking question—anything that will leave readers with something to think about or discuss.

AVOID A WEAK ENDING

Here's what you want to avoid in your conclusion:

DON'T introduce a new idea or afterthought that hasn't already been developed. That just leaves readers confused.

DON'T announce that you're going to conclude. We know that because there are no pages left.

DON'T apologize for your work. If you don't like it, fix it!

When Jocelyn drafted the conclusion to her memo on reducing employee turnover, she made every single one of the above mistakes. See if you can identify them in the following paragraph:

> Now I'd like to conclude by reminding you how important an issue this will be for our company. We've also got to do something about two other problems—people coming in late and people billing for too much overtime. Of course, given those problems, some people may not see high turnover as such an important issue. And they may be right. Nevertheless, we should do something about it. This may not be the most complete summary of all the possible solutions, but at least it's a beginning.

What a mess! When Jocelyn reread her first draft, she was so dissatisfied with the wishy-washy conclusion she'd written that she rewrote it right away. This time she really took the proverbial bull by both its proverbial horns. Here's her new, improved conclusion:

What is to be done about the problem of employee turnover? The compelling results of an employee survey clearly show that offering our staff a flex-time work option would make employees feel more comfortable with their work schedules. We have seen how problems that might arise as a result of flex-time could be solved. And we have seen statistics that show that, with flex-time, not only does turnover go down, but productivity goes up. In the light of what we now know, I strongly suggest that our next step is to work out the details of a flex-time schedule for our employees, and put the program into action as soon as possible.

That's much better. Go back to the list of different ways to write a good conclusion and see which ones Jocelyn used.

FELICIA WRITES A DRAFT

Here's the first draft of Felicia's personal essay on t'ai chi. Note that she starts with a good introduction, goes on to use several types of elaboration, and ends with a strong conclusion. We have left this sample "in the rough," so that in the next chapter you can see how Felicia revised and edited her draft.

Application to Ideal College

Question: "Tell us more about yourself in 250–500 words."

[Note: To make sure she focuses on her audience and her purpose, Felicia writes the question she is answering at the top of the page. It doesn't count as part of the 250–500 words.]

What I Learned from Studying T'ai Chi

Once a rather impatient boy went to study with a master. The day of the first lesson he handed him a piece of jade, and shut him in a room all by himself. When some time had passed the boy was released without a word. The day of the second lesson the same thing happened again. This continued on for several months until finally the pupil said "Now, look, Master. I wanted to study with you, and I've done everything you said. But you've taught me nothing. You've just locked me in a room and handed me a piece of jade every day. And today you gave me a piece of

jade that's a fake!" The Master answered, "If you've learned nothing, how did you know the jade was fake." In my t'ai chi class I was a lot like the pupil in the story. I didn't think I was making progress, then, just as I was getting impatient and ready to give up, I found that there was hope for me after all.

First of all, I expected to learn t'ai chi easily. I'm a good student, so I always think that anything will come easy to me. I guess you might call it a case of over-confidence. Second, I was sure I'd be the best student in the class. I usually am the best student in the class, and because I'm usually the best, I had come to think that being the best was the most important thing. Third, all my teachers all always telling me how good my work is, so I expected my t'ai chi teacher to be praising me all the time just like the others. I had come to think that praise, too, was very important. More important, even, than what I was learning!

My experience in t'ai chi, however, did not meet my expectations. I wasn't the best in the class. I felt awkward and clumsy, while other students moved with grace and ease. Instead of learning easily t'ai chi was very difficult for me. Finally, I wasn't praised by my teacher. In fact, I was criticized by him. One day he actually yelled at me in front of the whole class. "You must learn to have patience and concentrate!" These were the only words he said to me the whole first week of lessons. I felt humiliated and embarrassed. I wanted to give up right then and there.

But I didn't give up. I had a lot of determination, even though I had a lot of false expectations. I thought about what my teacher had said. I tried to have more patience and concentrate harder. I practiced and practiced. I practiced t'ai chi even more hours than my sister practices the piano. Finally my teacher noticed I was making progress. But what he said wasn't exactly praise: "Not so bad. Now work more!" Then he gave the whole class a speech about concentrating on learning instead of on being best. I knew he was talking about me.

I did work more—and more, and more. I improved, but my teacher never praised me. I came to understand that by not praising me, he was teaching something even more important than t'ai chi. He was teaching me that learning itself is its own reward. That was the first lesson I learned from t'ai chi. The second was that the most rewarding things in life don't come easily. Lesson number three was that being the best is not important. What is important is knowing that you worked your hardest and tried your best. But the most important thing I learned was to keep trying, even when it seems you may fail. Like the boy in the story, if a person concentrates and works hard, they are learning even if they don't know it. To concentration and hard work, add patience. The true reward is bound to follow.

Felicia breathes a huge sigh of relief. She knows her essay is not perfect—she can already see many things she would like to change. But the first big hurdle is over. In an ideal world, Felicia would have enough time to put her essay away for the rest of the day and come back to it with a fresh eye (and brain) the next day. But this world is not always ideal, so maybe she has waited until the last minute and the essay has to go into overnight mail tonight to make Ideal College's application deadline—tomorrow! We are still going to let her take just a little break before she gets down to the revising and editing that will turn her first rough draft into a final smooth and polished essay.

Plug In

Experiment with the different kinds of conclusions you have seen. To refresh your memory, here is a list of ideas discussed in this chapter:

- Summarize
- Restate
- Leave a strong impression
- Indicate a course of action
- Illustrate your main idea with an anecdote

Now, write a conclusion for the first draft of your essay or speech. After you're finished, look everything over. Can you believe it? You've got a complete piece of writing. Congrats!

ON TO THE NEXT STEP

We told you that once you had your outline, writing would be a piece of cake, and we think you'll find we were telling the truth—well, almost the truth. Why "almost"? Here comes the confession. Another term for "first draft" is "rough draft," and the word "rough" is the giveaway. Your finished piece of writing needs to be smooth. And do you see anyone around here—besides yourself—who's going to take your rough draft and smooth it out? No, we don't either. So you're going to have one more job after your first draft is finished—we call it the "repair job." The technical term is "revising and editing," the focus for the next section of *Writing Power*.

To Prepare for Revising Once the First Draft Is Written.　Once you've completed your first or rough draft, you've reached a major milestone in the writing process. We've already forecast the revising and editing to come. So how can you best prepare for this next phase? Our advice won't be too tough to abide by: Take a break!

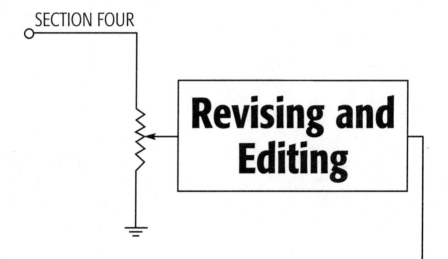

Revising and Editing

Polish Your Gem

You're almost there—but not quite. Don't say we didn't warn you. There's still some work to be done. Now you've got to smooth out that rough draft, polish that diamond in the rough. And that doesn't just mean correcting spelling or grammar mistakes. It means getting your words, sentences, and paragraphs to work together in the best possible way, the way that makes the most sense and that sounds the best, too. We will take you through the three stages of the revising and editing process. When you're finished—really finished, this time— you're going to like what you've done. So will the people who read it.

Warming Up. Look over this section before you start reading it in detail. Revision is the key to a manuscript that shines. Without good recrafting skills, your manuscript may appear mediocre, slipping by those who are reading it.

Stretching. You will find exercises throughout this section. Try them. They will give you good feedback on whether or not you are grasping the whole idea of clarifying your work and getting it the way you want it.

Working Out. Revise your own work as you go along. The chapters will tell you when to have another go at it. No one really gets it perfect the first, or even the second time. So give yourself the space and time you need to do an excellent job.

Training. Make sure you have someone who can look at your drafts as you get them done. Sometimes you are simply too close to your own work to spot mistakes or awkward phrasing. Pick that person carefully and reward them; perhaps with a lunch out, or an offer to reciprocate when they need some help on their own writing.

Sprint. When it comes to a final draft, dig in and get it done. It will go much faster than you think, especially since you have done so much work training and working out with those first drafts!

Marathon. Polish it up. Use your spell-checker and make sure your paragraphs and sentences are clear.

Cooling Down. Let your redraft sit. Go for a walk, go to a movie. Take your best friend, your partner, your kids, out to dinner. Get away from it for at least two days, if you can.

Personal Best. Look at the draft one last time. Make tiny changes: add a comma, underline a point you want to emphasize. Send it off, turn it in, whatever you are supposed to do with it. Then forget about it for a while. You have done all you can do. Congratulate yourself and plan your next project.

YOUR DIAMOND IN THE ROUGH

When miners first dig up a diamond, it looks like a dull hunk of rock. You need a trained eye to recognize this rough stone as a valuable jewel, and you need the trained hand of a jeweler to help your diamond make the journey from "rough" to sparkling.

⌁〰 POWER LINE 〰⌁

Revising is part of writing. Few writers are so expert that they can produce what they are after on the first try.

−E. B. White, *Elements of Style*

Your rough draft is like a diamond in the rough, and you are about to polish it up. That means you will be marking up your work, perhaps several times, noting words, phrases, even whole paragraphs to be cut out, added, moved, or changed.

The most efficient way to get through this process is by using proofreader's marks. These are the marks used by people who work with manuscripts full time, and they were developed so that very precise instructions about revisions could be passed along through all the stages of publishing a newspaper, magazine, or a book. We recommend that you use them because they are so useful for making corrections and changes that you will still understand an hour later. But it is your choice, of course. We have included them here so that, at the very least, you will understand what they mean. (We have simplified some of the marks to make them more practical for personal use, and we've left out some of the more technical ones that you won't need.)

PROOFREADER'S MARKS

¶   Begin new paragraph

    Delete (with line through all that is to be deleted)

⌒   Close up; delete space

    Delete and close up (use when deleting letters within a word)

stet   Let it stand (with dotted line under the text that is to be left to stand as it was originally)

trans   Transpose (with a line curved around the text that is to be transposed)

ital   Set in italic type (with text underlined thta is to be italicized)

rom   Set in roman (plain) type (circle the text to be set in roman type)

bf   Set in boldface type (with wavy line under text to be boldfaced)

caps   Capitalize letter (or three underscores under the letter(s) to be capitalized).

∧   Insert here

∧   Insert comma

∨   Insert apostrophe (or single quotation mark)

∨   Insert quotation marks

⊙   Insert period

?/   Insert question mark

⊙   Insert semicolon

⊙   Insert colon

=   Insert hyphen

$\frac{1}{m}$ or $\frac{1}{n}$ Insert dash

(/)   Insert parentheses

CHAPTER SIXTEEN

○**What Belongs?**

The first stage of revising is like cleaning out a closet. Some old clothes will stay, and some will be thrown out—and of course, some nice, new clothes will be added. (You'll probably do some organizing too, but that comes at Stage Two.) Now if your closet is a mess, and you're perfectly happy to leave it that way, who cares? No one has to see it but you. However, your writing is a different story—remember your audience? In this first stage, you'll figure out what does and doesn't belong in your work: what to leave alone, what to add, and what to cut.

> ∼〜〜○ **POWER LINE** ○〜〜〜∼
>
> Clarity, clarity, clarity! When you become hopelessly mired in a sentence, it is best to start fresh . . . . Usually what is wrong is that the construction has become too involved at some point; the sentence needs to be broken apart and replaced by two or more shorter sentences.
>
> —E. B. White, *Elements of Style*

REVISE BY CUTTING

As you reread your work, you may notice places where you repeated yourself, padded a sentence, or just went on and on. For instance, as we were revising the introduction to this section, we came across the following sentence:

> When miners first dig up a diamond it has an appearance closely resembling a dull hunk of rock.

This sentence is padded and overwritten. It is almost as if we had tried to use as many words as possible to take up more space. (*Us?*) How would you trim that padded, overwritten sentence down to size? Take out your pen and your proofreader's marks and get to work! Then check our version below to see how your edit compares with ours.

> When miners first dig up a diamond it looks like a dull hunk of rock.

How will you know when a sentence has too many words in it? By obeying the following nifty rule.

Cutting Extra Words

Remember this revising rule: If you can communicate the same idea in fewer words than you have used, do it!

In the above example we shortened "it has an appearance closely resembling" to "it looks like." Much better.

Sometimes a writer can't resist the urge to show off his or her knowledge, or just drop in some fascinating fact because it's, well, so fascinating. That's fine, we all have those urges. If you can't resist them when you are writing, make amends now. Cut out all the "fluff"—the irrelevant material that doesn't belong—no matter how fascinating.

Or you may find that you have written sentences or parts of sentences that just aren't necessary. For example, let's say we had written the following:

> When miners first dig up a diamond, ruby, emerald, or other precious gem, it looks like a dull hunk of rock.

It's a good thing we deleted the whole middle of that sentence from "ruby" through "gem." But how do you know when you've included stuff that doesn't belong? By remembering our next cutting rule.

Taking Out Unnecessary Material

You'll never go wrong if you abide by our "Three Golden Take-Outs":

- Take out words that don't relate to the main idea of a sentence
- Take out sentences that don't relate to the main idea of the paragraph
- Take out paragraphs that don't relate to the main idea (your thesis statement)

In the example above, all the business about emeralds and rubies didn't help make our point at all. The diamond comparison was enough. And enough is enough! Remember that the Three Golden Take-Outs can apply to whole sentences and even to whole paragraphs. If you find yourself rambling on, or rather rambling off your topic, it's time to start cutting.

REVISE BY ELABORATING

Revising by elaborating means to revise by adding words, sentences, or paragraphs. You cut when you've written too much; you elaborate when you need to write more. Writers elaborate for many reasons, but the most common is this: They think their readers know everything that they know themselves.

> **POWER LINE**
>
> The longest way round is usually the shortest way home, and the one truly reliable shortcut in writing is to choose words that are strong and sure-footed to carry the reader on his way.
>
> –E. B. White, *Elements of Style*

For example, here is the beginning of the first draft of Malcolm's personal essay. Like Felicia, he plans to send it to the Ideal College admissions committee. Read over Malcolm's work, picturing the people who might read it. Can you find three places where those readers might be confused? Mark those places. Then jot down the questions you'd like Malcolm to answer.

> Have you ever been completely surprised by a person you thought you knew? That's what happened to me in Mr. Ford's class. Mr. Ford was tough, but fair. And none of us ever talked back to him. Then one day, Roberto Suarez spoke up. Mr. Ford had given us an assignment. Roberto wanted to write about Mexico, instead. To our surprise, Mr. Ford agreed. We couldn't believe it! Roberto of all people.

Here are the three questions you'd probably like to ask Malcolm:

1. What grade and subject does Mr. Ford teach?
2. What assignment had he given?
3. Why was it surprising that Roberto, "of all people," would speak up?

Here's one way Malcolm might have revised by elaborating.

> Have you ever been completely surprised by a person you thought you knew? That's what happened to me in Mr. Ford's seventh-grade Social Studies class. Mr. Ford was tough, but fair. And none of us ever talked back to him.
>
> Then one day, Roberto Suarez did exactly that. He was a quiet boy who always sat in the back row, kept to himself, and never said much in class. Most of the students thought he wasn't very smart, and I am ashamed to admit that I was one of them. So we were all surprised when Mr. Ford assigned a term paper on European countries, and Roberto raised his hand to say, in no uncertain terms, that he wanted to write about Mexico, instead. To our further surprise, Mr. Ford agreed. We could not believe it! Roberto, of all people, having his own ideas about an assignment! We also couldn't understand why Mr. Ford was treating his ideas with such respect, since Roberto had always been such a poor student.

Now Malcolm's readers know what they need to know in order to follow the story. Note: A lot of these missing points were actually in Malcolm's outline. As he revises, he can compare his outline to his first draft to see what else he might have left out.

Know When to Elaborate

When should you elaborate? Just ask yourself these three questions:

1. Have I given readers all the information they need to understand my writing? Is there more background information my readers would need? Have I referred to people, places, or events of which readers might be unaware?

2. Have I given readers all the explanations they will need to understand my writing? Have I used words or phrases that need definitions? Have I mentioned names of people that need to be identified? (For example, if you mentioned "Mr. Maddox, my woodworking teacher" in paragraph 3, but he's just plain old "Mr. Maddox" in paragraph 1, your readers will probably be confused. Cross out the identification in paragraph 3 and write it in paragraph 1. Hey! You get to use those proofreading marks now!)

3. Are there additional points I should make? Have I made a strong case for my ideas? Are there any points that could support my ideas better? Can I anticipate a reader's possible arguments against my ideas? If so, can I answer those objections in advance?

ADD TRANSITIONS

One more way to improve your writing by elaboration is by adding transitions. Transitions are words or phrases that guide the reader from one idea to the next.

For example, read the two following pairs of sentences and see which is easier and more comfortable to read.

> **POWER LINE**
>
> The ease in writing comes from art, not chance.
>
> As those move easiest who have learned to dance.
>
> 'Tis not enough no harshness gives offence,
>
> The sound must seem an echo to the sense.
>
> —Alexander Pope

> Australia is home to many unusual animals. The platypus is a mammal, but lays eggs.

> Australia is home to many unusual animals. The platypus, for example, is a mammal, but lays eggs.

The sentences in the first pair seem to express two unrelated ideas until you, the reader, figure out that one sentence gives an example of the idea expressed by the other. In the second pair, the writer has done that job for you by simply adding the words "for example." You want to give your readers all the help you can. So, as you revise, add transitional words and phrases where needed.

The following page contains some common useful transitions.

Transitional Words and Phrases

Transitions that show you are adding an idea: *and, again, furthermore, equally, also, in addition, moreover*

Transitions that show you are giving an example: *for example, as, for instance, that is, like, in other words, such as*

Transitions that point out causes and effects: *because, so, thus, consequently, if . . . then, accordingly, therefore, as a result, since, for that reason, due to, owing to*

Transitions that point out comparisons (similarities): *in comparison, in the same way, also, similarly, likewise*

Transitions that point out contrasts (differences): *although, on the one hand, different from, yet, in contrast, nevertheless, however, but, unlike*

Transitions that show temporal order: *after, before, soon, since, once, later, when, finally, first, last, next, now, second, then, suddenly, whenever, third, until, as soon as, meanwhile, while, yesterday, during*

Transitions that show spatial order: *above, around, to the right, on top of, below, to the left, in front of, outside, where, behind, there, to the center, beside, here, near, across, opposite, next to, inside, along the side*

Transitions that show order of importance: *first, better, less important, third, last, weakest, most of all, best, second, most importantly, strongest, least important*

One word of caution. We don't mean that you have to use transitional words and phrases for all your sentences. That would be ridiculous. You have to figure out when a transition is necessary by asking yourself:

- Will the connections between my ideas be obvious to readers? If yes, then no transition is needed.
- Are the connections unclear? If yes, then add a transition.

YOUR TURN

Good old Felicia. Here's that rough draft she wrote back in the previous chapter. And here are your assignments:

1. Your next job is to make Stage One revisions on Felicia's draft. Use proofreader's marks to make your changes on the copy below.
2. Then read on to see our suggested second draft. Remember, you are looking for places to cut and elaborate.

There are other changes to make and mistakes to correct, too. Let them wait for Stage Two and Stage Three. If you can't stand passing over the mistakes, go ahead and fix them. But we'll be looking at the same draft in Stage Two, and the mistakes will still be there.

What I Learned from Studying T'ai Chi

Once a rather impatient boy went to study with a master. The day of the first lesson he handed him a piece of jade, and shut him in a room all by himself. When some time had passed the boy was released without a word. The day of the second lesson the same thing happened again. This continued on for several months until finally the pupil said "Now, look, Master. I wanted to study with you, and I've done everything you said. But you've taught me nothing. You've just locked me in a room and handed me a piece of jade every day. And today you gave me a piece of jade that's a fake!" The Master answered, "If you've learned nothing, how did you know the jade was fake." In my t'ai chi class I was a lot like the pupil in the story. I didn't think I was making progress, then, just as I was getting impatient and ready to give up, I found that there was hope for me after all.

First of all, I expected to learn t'ai chi easily. I'm a good student, so I always think that anything will come easy to me. I guess you might call it a case of over-confidence. Second, I was sure I'd be the best student in the class. I usually am the best student in the class, and because I'm usually the best, I had come to think that being the best was the most important thing. Third, all my teachers all always telling me how good my work is, so I expected my t'ai chi teacher to be praising me all the time just like the others. I had come to think that praise, too, was very important. More important, even, than what I was learning!

149

My experience in t'ai chi, however, did not meet my expectations. I wasn't the best in the class. I felt awkward and clumsy, while other students moved with grace and ease. Instead of learning easily t'ai chi was very difficult for me. Finally, I wasn't praised by my teacher. In fact, I was criticized by him. One day he actually yelled at me in front of the whole class. "You must learn to have patience and concentrate!" These were the only words he said to me the whole first week of lessons. I felt humiliated and embarrassed. I wanted to give up right then and there.

But I didn't give up. I had a lot of determination, even though I had a lot of false expectations. I thought about what my teacher had said. I tried to have more patience and concentrate harder. I practiced and practiced. I practiced t'ai chi even more hours than my sister practices the piano. Finally my teacher noticed I was making progress. But what he said wasn't exactly praise: "Not so bad. Now work more!" Then he gave the whole class a speech about concentrating on learning instead of on being best. I knew he was talking about me.

I did work more—and more, and more. I improved, but my teacher never praised me. I came to understand that by not praising me, he was teaching something even more important than t'ai chi. He was teaching me that learning itself is its own reward. That was the first lesson I learned from t'ai chi. The second was that the most rewarding things in life don't come easily. Lesson number three was that being the best is not important. What is important is knowing that you worked your hardest and tried your best. But the most important thing I learned was to keep trying, even when it seems you may fail. Like the boy in the story, if a person concentrates and works hard, they are learning even if they don't know it. To concentration and hard work, add patience. The true reward is bound to follow.

FELICIA'S SECOND DRAFT

What I Learned from Studying T'ai Chi

Once a master jeweler had an impatient pupil. The day of the first lesson he handed him a piece of jade, and shut him in a room. When two hours had passed the boy was released without a word. The day of the second lesson the same thing happened. This continued for several months until finally the pupil said "Now, look, Master. I wanted to study with you, and I've done everything you said. But you've taught me nothing. You've just locked me in a room and handed me a piece of jade ever day. And today you gave me a fake piece of jade!" The master answered, "If you've learned nothing, how did you know the jade was fake." In my t'ai chi class I was a lot like the pupil in the story. I didn't think I was making progress, then, just as I was getting impatient and ready to give up, I found that there was hope for me after all.

First of all, I expected to learn t'ai chi easily. I'm a good student, so I always think that anything will come easy to me. I guess you might call it a case of over-confidence. Second, I was sure I'd be the best student in the class. I usually am, and had therefore come to place tremendous importance upon being best. Third, my teachers praise my work so often that I expected praise from my t'ai chi teacher, as well. I had come to think that praise, too, was very important. More important, even, than what I was learning!

My experience in t'ai chi, however, did not meet my expectations. I wasn't the best in the class. I felt awkward and clumsy, while other students moved with grace and ease. Instead of learning easily, t'ai chi was very difficult for me. Finally, I wasn't praised by my teacher. In fact, I was criticized by him. One day he actually yelled at me in front of the class. "You must learn to have patience and concentrate!" These were the only words he said to me the whole first week of lessons. I felt humiliated and embarrassed. I wanted to give up right then and there.

But I didn't give up. I had a lot of determination, even though I had a lot of false expectations. I thought about what my teacher had said. I tried to have more patience and concentrate harder. I practiced and practiced. Finally my teacher noticed I was making progress. But what he said wasn't exactly praise: "Not so bad. Now work more!"

I did work more—and more, and more. I improved, but my teacher never praised me. I came to understand that by not praising me, he was teaching me something even more important than t'ai chi. He was teaching me that learning itself is its own reward. That was the first lesson I learned from t'ai chi. The second was that the most rewarding things in life don't come easily. I had more trouble learning t'ai chi than anything else I'd ever attempted, and yet I find it the most rewarding of my activities. Perhaps it is the great effort demanded by t'ai chi that makes it so rewarding. Lesson number three was that being the best is not important. What is important is knowing that you worked your hardest and tried your best. But the most important thing I learned was to keep trying, even when it seems you may fail. Like the boy in the story, if a person concentrates and works hard, they are learning even if they don't know it. To concentration and hard work, add patience. The true reward is bound to follow.

Plug In

Time to get out the first draft you wrote in Section Two and make your Stage One revisions.

Feel free to change anything that strikes you, but focus on improving your draft by cutting and elaborating. When you write for real, of course, you won't separate the three stages like this. You should go through each stage, but if you happen to see a mistake, you will probably correct it right then and there. Since this is a dry run, see if you can hold off with other corrections until Stage Two. For now, focus on these words: cut and elaborate!

CHAPTER SEVENTEEN

What is the Best Way to Express Myself?

In chapter 16, you revised your writing by cutting and elaborating. Now your first draft is your second draft. It is time to make changes on that second draft to see that your writing is smooth and polished. Your ideas need to be in a logical order so that they can be easily followed by your readers.

But first, go directly back to Section One and review the Four Golden Rules of writing. Do not pass Go. Do not collect $200. Then go over your work with those rules in mind. As you progress through Stage Two revisions, you will be looking:

- First at your work as a whole
- Then at your paragraphs
- Then at your sentences
- And finally at your words

Grammar, spelling, and punctuation all get checked in Stage Three. As you go, ask yourself these questions:

- Are my paragraphs in a logical order that the reader can easily follow?
- Are my sentences in the best order within each paragraph?
- Are my sentences varied? Do I start every paragraph with a question? Do three sentences in a row begin with *I*? Should I vary, combine, or break up sentences to make my work more interesting?
- Have I chosen the right words—the ones that convey both the idea and the feeling that I intend?

We'll take these questions one at a time. You can come back to this checklist every time you revise.

MAKE YOUR DRAFT COHERENT

The word *coherence* comes from two Latin roots that mean *together* (as in *cooperate*) and *stick* or *cling* (as in *adhesive*). Therefore the word literally means *stick together*. What does sticking together have to do with your writing? Plenty. Perhaps the most important writing skill you can develop is the ability to make a piece of writing hold together, so that the reader moves easily from one point to another without finding any gaps or places where he or she needs to stop and say, "Huh?"

Build Coherence in Your Draft. The first way to get rid of that "Huh?" problem is to read your work now to make sure the paragraphs flow in an order that makes sense and that transitions lead the reader from one paragraph to the next. Then make sure that the sentences within each paragraph flow smoothly as well.

Once you have done that, you have a coherent piece of writing—one that readers can read comfortably and easily. Instead of saying, "Huh?" they'll be saying, "Yeah, I get the point." We guess you get the point that coherence is a good thing.

Your Turn

In Stage One, you made sure that you included all the necessary information and cut out all the padding and fluff. That was good, but you are still not done. Now you have got to make sure that every sentence is in the right order. As an example, let's turn to Jocelyn, the personnel manager.

○⌇⌇⌇○ **POWER LINE** ○⌇⌇⌇○

Make the paragraph the unit of composition. The paragraph is a convenient unit; it serves all forms of literary work. As long as it holds together, a paragraph may be of any length–a single, short sentence or a passage of great duration.

–E. B. White, *Elements of Style*

Jocelyn is having trouble writing another memo. She is still grappling with the problem of reducing employee turnover, but this time she is evaluating extra personal days as an alternative to offering employees the option of flex-time schedules. (Wouldn't it be nice to have a job at *her* company?) As you will see, she is having a coherence problem.

We have numbered each sentence in this paragraph to help you think about the order. After you've said, "Huh?" a couple of times, figure out the order you think these sentences *should* be in.

(1) To decrease employee turnover, giving employees more personal days is an alternative to offering flex-time scheduling. (2) Flex-time is the best idea. (3) Adding one or two more personal days a year would not be as expensive as offering more vacation time. (4) Employees seem to like this idea. (5) Probably they would get one extra personal day after three years and another extra day after five years. (6) This idea is cheaper than added vacation time. (7) Flex-time is far more popular than extra personal days.

Whew! That paragraph is all over the place. You can almost hear Jocelyn's mind going back and forth as she wrestles with the problem. But readers don't want to share her confusion; they want her to help them understand what the problem is and what the company should do about it.

Help Jocelyn out! On a separate sheet of paper, rewrite her paragraph to make it more coherent.

Hint: Transitions can help bring coherence to a paragraph by showing the connection between two ideas. The transitions listed in the last chapter can help you choose the right words.

Second Hint: You will also have to rewrite at least two sentences and throw one out altogether. This is often the case. Rearranging sentences brings new writing problems to solve. The resulting coherence is well worth it, though.

Now compare your rewritten paragraph to ours. We have italicized the transitions we added.

(1) To decrease employee turnover, giving employees more personal days is an alternative to offering flex-time scheduling. (2) Although flex-time options are probably the most effective way to reduce employee turnover, there is another way. (3) *We might add* one or two more personal days a year. This would not be as expensive as offering more vacation time. (4) *Moreover,* employees seem to like this idea. (5) Probably they would get one extra personal day after three years and another extra day after five years. (7) *However,* tuition reimbursement is far more popular than extra personal days. (2) *Therefore,* tuition benefits seem to be the best idea for our company.

As you can see, we made Jocelyn's paragraph more coherent by addressing first one side of the argument—how personal days would work. Then we addressed the other—why flex-time is still a better plan. Transitions helped readers follow each argument. They showed whether the next sentence was adding to the argument ("Moreover") or contradicting it ("However").

Before we move on to writing effective sentences, one more point about order and coherence: If Jocelyn goes on to write another paragraph elaborating on this one, she should *keep her points in the same order,* writing about personal days first, then about flex-time. Changing the order can confuse readers, and confusing readers is not a good thing.

⌐⌐⌐ **POWER LINE** ⌐⌐⌐

We like that a sentence should read as if its author, had he held a plough instead of a pen, could have drawn a furrow deep and straight to the end.

—Henry David Thoreau

ADD SENTENCE VARIETY

So you've gotten your paragraphs in order by putting your sentences into a logical order that is easy to follow. Now, look at your sentences. Do they all sound alike? If you find you are beginning every sentence with the same word, or even with the subject, you may be putting your readers to sleep. Writing sentences that are all the same length is yet another way of lulling your readers into a stupor. While that's not as bad as confusing them, it's not a good thing, either.

To Add Sentence Variety to Your Draft. Here are some ways to keep your readers awake with a pleasing array of sentence variety:

- Begin some sentences with words other than the subject.
- Throw in a few longer sentences and some short ones to vary the rhythm.
- Write different types of sentences. Throw in a question or an exclamation once in a while. (*Once in a while,* we said. That means *not too often.*)

Ralph, the guy who started out writing about Victorian women and then did a report on the novel *Jane Eyre,* wrote the following introductory sentences and then revised them:

> *Jane Eyre* is a novel written by Charlotte Brontë and published in 1847. The main character is a young woman who comes to work for a wealthy family. She finds herself involved in a perplexing mystery as well as a passionate romance.

Each of Ralph's sentences begins with the subject. Moreover, (nice transition there!) each one is approximately the same length. His revision might not be the most thrilling piece of prose you've ever read, but it is less of a snooze:

> Written by Charlotte Brontë and published in 1847, *Jane Eyre* is a novel about a young woman who comes to work for a wealthy family. She finds herself involved in a perplexing mystery as well as a passionate romance.

Note that Ralph made only two simple changes. First he noodled with the first sentence so it begins with words other than the subject. Then he combined it with the second sentence to make it longer, in contrast to the shorter final sentence, which he wisely left alone. Ralph could spice up the entire book report with just one exclamation, *if appropriate,* but those are to be used very sparingly. (They lose effect and get silly if used too often.)

COMBINE SENTENCES

You just noticed that Ralph combined two sentences into one. Sentence combining is a wonderful technique for curing many writing ills. As you have seen, it is a good way to vary the length of your sentences. It is also a way to avoid choppy sounding or repetitious writing. Here is an example from Ralph's book report:

> **Separate, Choppy, Repetitious:** St. John Rivers wants to be a missionary. He is a virtuous man. He is also cold.

> **Combined, Smoother, Repetition Avoided:** St. John Rivers, who wants to be a missionary, is a virtuous but cold man.

Your Turn

How would you avoid repetition and combine and smooth out these sentences? Write your new and improved version on the line provided.

> Jane admires St. John Rivers. She respects him a great deal. She does not want to marry him.

_____

Here is our combined version:

> Jane greatly admires and respects St. John Rivers, but she does not want to marry him.

BREAK UP SENTENCES

At one point in his second draft, Ralph thought that he had written too many short, choppy sentences. So he made the opposite mistake and began writing long sentences that were hard to follow. Read on and see what we mean.

> When Jane runs away from Rochester, she crosses the moors alone at night, then collapses, and luckily is rescued by two sisters, Mary and Diana Rivers.

In Stage Two revision, Ralph broke that sentence up:

When Jane runs away from Rochester, she crosses the moors alone at night. Then she collapses. Luckily, she is rescued by two sisters, Mary and Diana Rivers.

Notice that Ralph's sentences are not only easier to understand, they are varied in length (one short sentence in between two longer ones) and structure (each one begins in a different way).

Your Turn

Here is another too-long sentence from Ralph's paper. How would you break it up?

> **Too Long:** The Rivers sisters care for Jane, nurse her back to health, and become her friends, although their housekeeper is suspicious of Jane at first, but eventually she, too, comes to love and trust Jane.

Here is one suggested revision:

> The Rivers sisters care for Jane and nurse her back to health. Although their housekeeper is suspicious of Jane at first, the sisters become Jane's friend. Eventually, the housekeeper comes to love and trust Jane, as well.

But when Ralph looked at that paragraph again, he wasn't quite happy with the second sentence. The relationship between the sisters' kind feelings towards Jane and the housekeeper's suspicion is kind of vague. Now that Ralph has broken up his original sentence, he sees the need to express his ideas more clearly. Here is his next revision:

> The Rivers sisters care for Jane and nurse her back to health. They become her friends, but Jane still has one enemy in their house: the housekeeper. Eventually, however, she, too, comes to love and trust Jane.

Now, on a separate piece of paper, hone your revising skills while helping Ralph improve yet another paragraph from the second draft in his essay. Feel free to change any words you like.

> Jane thinks she is very plain. All her life she has been plain. Then she meets Mr. Rochester. He does not think she is plain. Or if he does, he does not care. Mr. Rochester knows many beautiful women. One of them, Blanche Ingram, acts as though she and Mr. Rochester are engaged, and she is also very insulting to Jane, so that Jane is hurt and jealous. Then Jane discovers that Mr. Rochester loves her.

Here is our suggested revision. Compare it to yours . . .

> All her life, Jane has believed she is plain. Then she meets Mr. Rochester, who either does not consider her plain or does not care. However, Mr. Rochester knows many beautiful women. One in particular, Blanche Ingram, acts as though she and Mr. Rochester are engaged. She insults Jane, who is hurt and jealous. Then Jane discovers that Mr. Rochester loves her, and not Blanche.

As you can see, we had to change a few words here and there. Did you do the same? Do you know why? Whose choices did you like better, yours or ours? Why? Thinking about these questions will help you develop your own writing style.

POWER LINE

The difference between the right word and the almost right word is the difference between lightning and the lightning bug.

—Mark Twain

CHOOSE EFFECTIVE WORDS

Have you ever played the following word game?

> *I* am svelte. *You* are thin. *He* is skinny.

> *I* am thrifty. *You* are frugal. *She* is just plain stingy!

What gives the game its punch is its play on *connotations,* or the shades of meaning that many words convey beyond their dictionary definitions. Technically, *thrifty, frugal,* and *stingy* all apply to someone who does not spend money easily. But *thrifty* connotes, or suggests, someone who is wise and careful with his or her money. *Frugal* implies that a person doesn't have very much money and therefore does not spend much. *Stingy,* of course, suggests a person who has money and meanly chooses not to spend or share it.

Likewise, *svelte* connotes glamour, *thin* is a fairly neutral word, and *skinny* suggests a criticism.

When you revise your writing, make sure each word you have chosen implies just the right shade of meaning. For example, Ralph, in his history paper on Victorian women, wrote the following sentence:

> Victorian women's courageous struggle to win their rightful place in society led to many hardships—and many victories.

Ralph intended to portray Victorian women in a favorable light, so he used many words that have *positive connotations:* courageous, struggle, rightful, victories. Even "hardships" has a noble ring in this context. Ralph's classmate, Celia, was far more critical of Victorian women. Here is what she wrote in her paper on the same topic:

> Victorian women's pathetic scramble for a more favored place in society led to inevitable hardship—as well as to an occasional victory.

Although Celia is describing the same events as Ralph, her choice of words suggest that Victorian women were foolish and perhaps selfish. That is because of the words she used with *negative connotations:* pathetic, scramble, favored. Like Ralph, Celia speaks of "hardship," but in her essay, it is *inevitable* hardship—suggesting that the hardship was in some way the women's own fault. Celia also speaks of "victory," but by pointing out that it only "occasional," she makes it seem a small and not very worthwhile achievement.

Sometimes a connotation is inappropriate, not because it's inappropriately positive or negative but just because it's wrong. For example, Jocelyn had to write a stern memo about employees who were filling out their time cards incorrectly. She wrote:

> This type of *nonchalance* makes life more difficult for all of us.

"Nonchalance" isn't quite the right word here. It implies a devil-may-care attitude, a kind of breezy, cheerful disregard for consequences. That is not the image that Jocelyn wants to convey. Here is her revision:

> This type of *carelessness* makes life more difficult for all of us.

That's better! "Carelessness" puts the focus not on a cheerful, breezy attitude, but on a sloppy way of doing things. In fact, Jocelyn considers "sloppiness" for a moment:

> This type of *sloppiness* makes life more difficult for all of us.

Nope. That word, with its strong negative connotation, is too harsh for the situation. It will offend workers, rather than encourage them to mend their ways (even if they are sloppy). Jocelyn goes back to "carelessness."

Often, it's difficult to say just *why* one word feels right and another feels wrong. But if you pay attention, both to what you write and to what you read and hear, you will probably realize that you have a pretty good idea of what different words imply. You will sense their connotations and know when one *feels right*.

POWER LINE

Good writing is supposed to evoke sensation in the reader—not the fact that it's raining, but the feel of being rained upon.

—E. L. Doctrow

CHOOSE VIVID WORDS

Here are a few rules of thumb when it comes to choosing words:

- Specific is usually better than general. "Moose," for example, conjures up a picture in your mind right away, while "animal" leaves you blank.
- Concrete is usually better than abstract.

Abstract words cannot be perceived through the senses: love, democracy, sorrow. Concrete words can be perceived through the senses: kisses, ballot box, tears. Concrete words are more likely to conjure up a vivid picture in the reader's mind.

To Write Vividly. Details that appeal to the senses of sight, hearing, smell, taste, and touch, are the most specific concrete words of all. They can really make a piece of writing come to life.

Of course, if you are writing a paper on the importance of democracy, you will have to use that word at least once or twice. And if you are writing a paper on the environment, you may have to write something like: "This measure is harmful to animals," rather than, "This measure is harmful to moose, deer, elk, bear, panthers, etcetera, etcetera, etcetera." Still, whenever you can be more specific, concrete, and sensory, seize the chance.

Here is how Margarita tightened up her word choice in her second draft essay about Grandma Rose.

First draft version:

> Grandma Rose was a midwife in Italy for about five years before she came over to the United States. As a midwife to poor country-dwellers, she delivered many babies under extremely difficult conditions. When she came to New York City, she continued to work as a midwife, delivering babies for poor residents of the city.

Second draft version:

> Grandma Rose was a midwife in Italy for about five years before she made the long, seasick voyage to the United States. As a midwife to peasants living in rude shacks with dirt floors, she delivered many babies without having access to running water, clean sheets, or electric light. When she came to New York City, she continued to work as a midwife, delivering babies for women living in crowded, smelly tenement apartments.

As you can see, the revised version gives you a *vivid* image of Grandma Rose's life, which also helps you imagine the sort of person she must have been.

Your Turn

Here is another one of Margarita's second-draft paragraphs. Help Margarita revise it:

1. Replace words that have the wrong connotation.
2. Make abstract and general words specific and concrete.
3. Add sensory details where appropriate.

Since you don't know Margarita's family, feel free to make up specific images if necessary. The words you might want to change are in *italics*. (By the way, if you want to use a dictionary or thesaurus to help you, feel free!)

Margarita's second draft:

Then Grandma Rose *experienced* her first *giant* tragedy. Her oldest son, Enzo, *expired* at the age of only nine months. Grandma Rose was *very sad*. *Luckily*, she soon had another child, my Uncle Pietro, who was a *handsome* baby. Grandma used to *drag* Pietro with her everywhere, even to *the homes of her clients*. Grandma would deliver a new baby while Pietro played *carelessly* on the floor.

Your revision:

_____

_____

_____

_____

_____

_____

Here is one possible revision:

> Then Grandma Rose faced her first big tragedy. Her oldest son, Enzo, died at the age of only nine months. Grandma Rose cried for days. To her great joy, she soon had another child, my Uncle Pietro, a beautiful baby with big brown eyes and long black curls. Grandma used to carry Pietro with her everywhere, even to the tiny apartments of her customers. Grandma would deliver a new baby while Pietro played cheerfully on the linoleum floor.

YOUR TURN

Let's welcome Felicia back into our midst and join her as she does her Stage Two revisions. Once again, feel free to correct any errors you find, but remember you'll get a crack at proofreading for spelling, grammar, and punctuation errors in Stage Three. When you are done, compare your work to our revised draft.

What I Learned from Studying T'ai Chi

Once a master jeweler had an impatient pupil. The day of the first lesson he handed him a piece of jade, and shut him in a room. When two hours had passed the boy was released without a word. The day of the second lesson the same thing happened. This continued for several months until finally the pupil said "Now, look, Master. I wanted to study with you, and I've done everything you said. But you've taught me nothing. You've just locked me in a room and handed me a piece of jade every day. And today you gave me a fake piece of jade!" The master answered, "If you've learned nothing, how did you know the jade was fake." In my t'ai chi class I was a lot like the pupil in the story. I didn't think I was making progress, then, just as I was getting impatient and ready to give up, I found that there was hope for me after all.

First of all, I expected to learn t'ai chi easily. I'm a good student, so I always think that anything will come easy to me. I guess you might call it a case of over-confidence. Second, I was sure I'd be the best student in the class. I usually am, and had therefore come to place tremendous importance upon being best. Third, my teachers praise my work so often that I expected praise from my t'ai chi teacher, as well. I had come to think that praise, too, was very important. More important, even, than what I was learning!

My experience in t'ai chi, however, did not meet my expectations. I wasn't the best in the class. I felt awkward and clumsy, while other students moved with grace and ease. Instead of learning easily, t'ai chi was very difficult for me. Finally, I wasn't praised by my teacher. In fact, I was criticized by him. One day he actually yelled at me in front of the class. "You must learn to have patience and concentrate!" These were the only words he said to me the whole first week of lessons. I felt humiliated and embarrassed. I wanted to give up right then and there.

But I didn't give up. I had a lot of determination, even though I had a lot of false expectations. I thought about what my teacher had said. I tried to have more patience and concentrate harder. I practiced and practiced. Finally my teacher noticed I was making progress. But what he said wasn't exactly praise: "Not so bad. Now work more!"

I did work more—and more, and more. I improved, but my teacher never praised me. I came to understand that by not praising me, he was teaching me something even more important than t'ai chi. He was teaching me that learning itself is its own reward. That was the first lesson

166   **KAPLAN**

I learned from t'ai chi. The second was that the most rewarding things in life don't come easily. I had more trouble learning t'ai chi than anything else I'd ever attempted, and yet I find it the most rewarding of my activities. Perhaps it is the great effort demanded by t'ai chi that makes it so rewarding. Lesson number three was that being the best is not important. What is important is knowing that you worked your hardest and tried your best. But the most important thing I learned was to keep trying, even when it seems you may fail. Like the boy in the story, if a person concentrates and works hard, they are learning even if they don't know it. To concentration and hard work, add patience. The true reward is bound to follow.

FELICIA'S THIRD DRAFT

What I Learned from Studying T'ai Chi

Once a master jeweler had an impatient pupil. The day of the first lesson the Master handed his pupil a piece of jade, and shut him in a room. When two hours had passed he released the boy without a word. The day of the second lesson the same thing happened. This continued for several months until finally the pupil said "Now, look, Master. I wanted to study with you, and I've done everything you said. But you've taught me nothing. You've just handed me a piece of jade and locked me in a room every day. And today you gave me a fake piece of jade!" The master answered, "If you've learned nothing, how did you know the jade was fake." In my t'ai chi class I was much like the pupil in the story. I did not think I was making progress, then, just as I was getting impatient and ready to give up, I found that there was hope for me after all.

My difficulties in t'ai chi class all came from one central problem. Like the boy in the story, I let my impatience for what I considered to be success get in the way of my actual learning. First of all, I expected to learn t'ai chi easily. Being a good student, I always think that learning any subject will come easily to me. Second, I was sure I would be the best student in the class. Because I usually am, I had come to place tremendous importance upon being best. Third, my teachers praise my work so often that I expected praise from my t'ai chi teacher, as well. I had come to think that praise, too, was very important. In fact, praise had become even more important to me than what I was learning!

My experience in t'ai chi, however, did not meet my expectations. Instead of being easy to learn, t'ai chi was very difficult for me. I was not the best in the class. I felt awkward and clumsy, while other students moved with grace and ease. Finally, I was not praised by my teacher. In fact, I was criticized by him. One day he actually yelled at me in front of the class. "You must learn to have patience and concentrate!" These were the only words he said to me the whole first week of lessons. I felt humiliated and embarrassed. I wanted to give up right then and there.

But I didn't give up. I had the determination to keep trying, in spite of my many false expectations. I thought about what my teacher had said. I tried to have more patience and concentrate harder. I practiced and practiced. Finally my teacher noticed I was making progress. But what he said wasn't exactly praise: "Not so bad. Now work more!"

I did work more—and more, and more. I found that the most rewarding things in life do not come easily. I had more trouble learning t'ai chi than anything else I had ever attempted, and yet I find it the most rewarding of my activities. Perhaps it is the great effort demanded by t'ai chi that makes it so rewarding. That was the first thing I learned in t'ai chi. The second was that being the best is not important. It is more important for students of any subject to know that they worked their hardest and tried their best. Finally, I improved, but my teacher never praised me. I came to understand that by not praising me, he was teaching me something even more important than t'ai chi. He was teaching me that learning itself is the true reward. But the most important thing I learned was to keep trying, even in the face of possible failure. Like the boy in the story, if a person concentrates and works hard, he or she is learning even if success is not immediately apparent. In other words, to concentration and hard work, add patience. The true reward is bound to follow.

Plug In

Get your second draft and do your Stage Two revisions to it. Feel free to change anything that strikes you. This time focus on:

- Making your paragraphs coherent
- Making your sentences varied, smooth, and easy to understand
- Keeping your word choice precise and vivid

CHAPTER EIGHTEEN

What Mistakes Have I Made?

At last you've completed a piece of writing that you're happy with—happy enough to prepare a final draft. *Proofreading*, Stage Three in revising and editing your writing, is your final chance to correct errors in spelling, grammar, usage, capitalization, and punctuation.

LOOK FOR COMMON MISTAKES

Here are some of the most common mistakes that have plagued writers the world over from time immemorial. So if you have to make corrections, welcome to the club.

Incorrect Words and Phrases Hit List. Here's a handy list for every writer: incorrect words and phrases, and how to fix them. This hodgepodge wins the Kaplan award for the most-often made writing mistakes. If you are aware of them, you can avoid them.

ain't—Unless you use are reproducing dialogue, use *am not, is not, isn't, are not, or aren't.*

could of—The words may sound like that. Really, though, the phrase is *could have.*

irregardless, disregardless—No such words. Use *regardless.*

graduate high school (or college)—This one is nit-picking, but you don't want to offend any college admissions people who are sticklers for grammar. The correct phrase is *graduate* from *high school (or college).*

anywheres, nowheres—No such words. Use *anywhere, nowhere.*

off of—That extra *of* is redundant. Instead of staying "He climbed off of the mechanical bull," just say, "He climbed off the mechanical bull."

alright—No such word. Use *all right.*

AVOID CONFUSING DOUBLES

Confusing doubles are words that are often confused with one another. If you know what each word means, you will remember how and when to use it.

> **POWER LINE**
>
> What is written without effort is in general read without pleasure.
>
> —Samuel Johnson

That/Which. "That" and "which" are confusing doubles, and the pair is one of the toughest calls in the English language. It is made more confusing by the fact that the British have different rules for this pair than do we Americans. Unlike *ain't,* which is virtually never misused by published writers, *that* and *which* are often used incorrectly, even in respectable academic journals. However, there is a correct usage, and an explanation. It gets a bit complicated, so follow us closely.

Both *that* and *which* introduce words that pertain to another word that came previously. In both sentences below, the italicized words describe the word *computer:*

> The computer *that* I use has broken down.

> The computer, *which* is such a wonderful invention, has made my work so much easier.

172

In the first sentence the phrase "that I use" lets the reader know I am talking only about one particular computer—the one I use. If you took out the phrase, the sentence would lose an important part of its meaning. The reader would have to ask, "which computer?" In this kind of sentence, *that* is correct.

In the second sentence, the phrase "which I use every day" adds information, but the information is not essential to the meaning of the sentence. It does not restrict the meaning of the word "computer" to just one computer. Here are some more examples:

> The coffeemaker *that* is on the tenth floor makes great coffee!

> The coffeemaker, *which* is on the tenth floor, makes great coffee!

These two sentences are good examples because they are exactly the same except for the words *that* and *which*. (If you're observant, you will notice one more difference: There are commas around the phrase "which is on the tenth floor" in the second sentence.) Actually, the two sentences have different meanings. The first means that there are coffeemakers on other floors, but the one on the tenth floor is the one to use because it, as opposed to the others, makes great coffee. The second sentence means that there is just one coffee maker in the building, and it makes great coffee. And, by the way, it's on the tenth floor.

Here's one more example:

> The report *that* I wrote is being published.

> The report, *which* I wrote, is being published.

Almost the same words, but different meanings. Sentence one tells us that one specific report, the one I wrote, is being published. In sentence two, we all know which report we're talking about. It's being published—and by the way, I wrote it.

If the words "by the way" make sense, use *which*. If they don't, use *that*. And as you might have guessed, a *which*-phrase takes a comma before and after it, but a *that*-phrase does not.

Who/Whom. People have somehow gotten the mistaken notion that *whom* is a more cultured word, and that it should be used whenever a more formal tone is needed. Actually, *who/whom* corresponds exactly to *he/him*. Whenever you would use *he*, use *who*. Whenever you'd use *him*, use *whom*.

I told *him* my deepest secret.

Whom did you tell your darkest secret?

He is going on the company picnic.

Who is going on the company picnic?

Do you think *he* is right for the job?

Who do you think is right for the job?

Do you want *him* for the job?

Whom do you want for the job?

Then/Than. *Then* has several meanings:

- *At that time,* as in "Soon it will be noon. *Then* I'll go to lunch."
- *Next,* as in "I'll go first, *then* you can go."
- *Immediately* or *soon afterward,* as in "The rain stopped, *then* started again."
- *In addition,* as in, "I love my job, and *then* it pays so well."
- *Therefore,* since that is so, as in, "Why, *then,* do you want to change it?"

Than is used to make comparisons:

Do you love me more *than* he does?

I did love you more *than* life itself, but *then* I realized that you were all wrong for me.

Affect/Effect. Okay, all together now. *Affect* is the verb; *effect* is the noun. Or, for the less grammatically minded, *affect* is the action, *effect* is the result:

> He could not *affect* me, but I had a big *effect* on him.

Looking for an easy way to remember the difference between the two words? Memorize the sentence above, changing *He* to *She* if you prefer. Also remember that *affect* and *effect* appear in that sentence in alphabetical order—*a* comes before *e*. Then say that sentence to yourself whenever you have to choose between the two words.

Farther/Further. *Farther* refers to distance. Literally, it means *more far,* as in:

> The castle you see is ten miles *farther* down the road.
>
> I was exhausted and could go no *farther.*

Further means *additional* or *more:*

> Do you have any *further* points to make?
>
> I won't discuss it any *further*!

To remember the difference, just look for the word *far.* Tell yourself: I can go *far* and *farther.*

I, He, She/Me, Him, Her. Grammatically speaking, *I, he,* and *she* are in the subjective case and are used to show who is acting; *me, him,* and *her* are in the objective case and are used to show who is acted upon, or who "receives" action.

> *I* love *her.*
>
> *She* hates *me.*
>
> *I* gave the book to *her.*
>
> *She* took the book from *me.*

Here's a tricky example. If someone asks you who is on the phone, you might say, "Is that *her*?" But since you would not say, "Yes, *her* is on the phone," you should really say, "Is that *she*?" "Yes," is the answer, "*she* is on the phone." Most people outside of British films don't say "Was that *she*?" but technically, they should. And since, in writing, the rules tend to be stricter, so should you.

Me/I. "Between you and *me*," is a phrase that causes a lot of confusion. Yes, we know some of you want to say, "between you and *I*," but *between* is a preposition and *me* is its object. Just memorize it: Any time the word *between* is used, *me*, *him*, or *her* are the words that should follow.

Than Her/Than She. Look at these two sentences:

> I like Jose better *than her.*

> Jose is a better candidate for the position *than she.*

It just doesn't seem fair that both of these sentences should be correct! But they are. How can you tell? Fill in the extra words:

> I like Jose better *than* (I like) *her.*

> Jose is a better candidate for the position than *she* (is).

Our advice? When you're using *than* plus a pronoun, fill in the extra words in your own mind. Then you'll know which pronoun to use.

Your Turn

If a word is used incorrectly in the following sentences, cross it out and write the correct word in its place. If a sentence has no mistakes, then leave it alone. And by all means, feel free to look back in this chapter for help, just as you would do if you were really revising your work. Hint: Many sentences have more than one incorrect word.

1. Irregardless of the results, taking the survey has had a positive affect on employee morale.

2. Now we know how many employees have graduated high school and how many have graduated from college.

3. We could of kept the results between you and I, but Mr. Farber wanted to publish them.

4. Whom do you think would of taken his place if he had left?

5. He is quite happy here; he is going nowheres.

6. He has been promoted quite quickly; he won't go farther for quite a while.

7. He has been here longer then her.

8. Attention, employees: Please clear all non-work-related materials off of your desks by Monday morning.

9. This is the memo that concerns me.

10. The mail which was delivered this morning arrived two hours late.

Here are our suggested revisions:

1. *Regardless* of the results, taking the survey has had a positive *effect* on employee morale.

2. Now we know how many employees have graduated *from* high school and how many have graduated from college.

3. We could *have* kept the results between you and *me,* but Mr. Farber wanted to publish them.

4. *Who* do you think would *have* taken his place if he had left?

5. He is quite happy here; he is going *nowhere.*

6. He has been promoted quite quickly; he won't go *further* for quite a while.

7. He has been here longer then *she has.*

8. Attention, employees: Please clear all non-work-related materials *off* your desks by Monday morning.

9. This is the memo that concerns me. (This sentence is correct.)

10. The mail *that* was delivered this morning arrived two hours late.

TIME TO PROOFREAD

Now it's time to go over your copy with a fine-tooth comb. Here are some suggestions:

- Exchange papers with a friend—it can be painful to identify your own errors but kind of fun to catch somebody else's.
- Read your work aloud. That way, you have to look at every word.
- Read your work backward, from the last word to the first. That way, you'll focus on how words look and not on what the writing sounds like.
- Proofread more than once. The first time, look for grammar problems; the second time, spelling errors; the third time capitalization, and so on.

Proofreading Checklists

These checklists can help you proofread your work. Refer back to the items each time you review your drafts.

Spelling Checklist

- Make sure you have spelled the names of people and places correctly.
- Check words with silent letters, such as *sophomore* and *spaghetti.*
- Double-check words that sound alike but are spelled differently, such as *there/they're/their, to/two/too,* and *its/it's.*
- Check contractions. Are the apostrophes in the right place?
- Check words that don't sound the way they are spelled.
- Look for words that are misspelled because they are mispronounced (*library, mischievous,* and *separate,* for example).
- Check the spelling of words from other languages, if necessary. Reminder: Even if you use a computer spell-checker, you must proofread! Your spell-checker won't pick up a spelling mistake if the mistake results in a real word. ("I saw a *many* and a woman standing on the corner.")

Grammar Checklist

- Make sure that each sentence expresses at least one complete idea.
- Be sure that the two parts of a compound sentence are correctly joined with a comma and a connecting word.
- Check all verbs to be sure they are in the correct form.
- Be sure that singular subjects have singular verbs, while plural subjects have plural verbs.
- Be sure that you do not mix singular and plural pronouns incorrectly. Wrong: A person (singular) should never forget their (plural) manners. Right: People (plural) should never forget their (plural) manners. A person (singular) should never forget her or his (singular) manners.
- Check your use of *me, him, her/I, he, she*

Capitalization Checklist

- Be sure to capitalize the first word of every sentence.
- Check the first word of every quotation. Is it capitalized?
- Capitalize the names of proper nouns: specific people, places, buildings, languages, nationalities, seasons, historical periods, organizations, religious terms, and initials.

Punctuation Checklist

- Be sure to end each sentence with an end mark such as a period, question mark, or exclamation point.
- Check for apostrophes in contractions and where needed to show ownership (but not in words like *hers* and *theirs*).
- See if you have begun and ended a speaker's direct words with quotation marks.
- Check to make sure you have used commas correctly, especially in a series of three or more items.
- Put words from other languages in italics (or underline them).

YOUR TURN

Help Felicia one last time by getting her third draft into its final form. This time, correct every single mistake you see. It's her last shot at this essay, and you would not want to let her down! Remember that, while you will be focusing on spelling, grammar, and punctuation errors, Stage Three is also the time to catch any mistakes you missed earlier on. We included only a few Stage Three errors in Felicia's essay because we didn't want the mistakes to distract you. It would be unfair if we neglected to tell you now that we've added some grammar, spelling, and punctuation errors for you to catch. Sorry . . .

What I Learned from Studying T'ai Chi

Once a master jeweler had an impatient pupil. The day of the first lesson the Master handed his pupil a peice of jade, and shut him in a room. When two hours had passed he released the boy without a word. The day of the second lesson the same thing happened. This continued for several months until finally the pupil said "Now, look, Master. I wanted to study with you, and I've done everything you said. But you've tauhgt me nothing. You've just handed me a piece of jade and locked me in a room every day. And today you gave me a fake piece of jade!" The master answered, "If you've learned nothing, how did you know the jade was fake." In my ta'i chi class I was much like the pupil in the story. I did not think I was making progress, then, just as I was getting impatient and ready to give up, I found that there was hope for me after all.

My difficulties in t'ai chi class all came from one central problem. Like the boy in the story, I let my impatience for what I considered to be success get in the way of my actual learning. First of all I expected to learn t'ai chi easily. Being a good student, I always think that learning any subject will come easily to me. Second, I was sure I would be the best student in the class. Because I usually am, I had come to place tremendous importance upon being best. Third, my teachers praise my work so often that I expected praise from my ta'i chi teacher, as well. I had come to think that praise, too, was very important. In fact, praise had become even more important to me then what I was learning!

My experience in t'ai chi, however, did not meet my expectations. Instead of being easy to learn, t'ai chi was very difficult for me. I was not the best in the class. I felt awkward and clumsy, while other students moved with grace and ease. Finally, I was not praised by my teacher. In fact, I was criticized by him. One day he actually yelled at me in front of the class. "You must learn to have patience, and concentrate!" These were the only words he said to me the whole first week of lessons. I felt humiliated and embarassed. I wanted to give up right then and there.

But I didn't give up. I had the determination to keep trying, in spite of my many false expectations. I thought about what my teacher had said. I tried to have more patience and concentrate harder. I practiced and practiced. Finally my teacher noticed I was making progress. But what he said wasn't exactly praise: "Not so bad. Now work more!"

I did work more—and more, and more. I found that the most rewarding things in life do not come easily. I had more trouble learning t'ai chi than anything else I had ever attempted, and yet I find it the most rewarding of my activities. Perhaps it is the great effort demanded by t'ai chi that makes it so rewarding. That was the first thing I learned in t'ai chi. The second was that being the best is not important. It is more important for students of any subject to know that they worked there hardest and tried their best. Finally, I improved, but my teacher never praised me. I came to understand that by not praising me, he was teaching me something even more important than t'ia chi. He was teaching me that learning itself is the true reward. But the most important thing I learned was to keep trying, even in the face of possible failure. Like the boy in the story, if a person concentrates and works hard, they are learning even if success is not immediately apparent. In other words, to concentration and hard work, add patience. The true reward is bound to follow.

FELICIA'S FINAL DRAFT

Here's a final version Felicia is happy with. Compare it with your final version.

What I Learned from Studying T'ai Chi

Once a master jeweler had an impatient pupil. The day of the first lesson the master handed his pupil a piece of jade, and shut him in a room. When two hours had passed he released the boy without a word. The day of the second lesson the same thing happened. This continued for several months until finally the pupil said, "Now, look, Master. I wanted to study with you, and I've done everything you said. But you've taught me nothing. You've just handed me a piece of jade and locked me in a room every day, and today you gave me a fake piece of jade!" The master answered, "If you've learned nothing, how did you know the jade was fake?" In my t'ai chi class I was much like the pupil in the story. I did not think I was making progress. Then, just as I was getting impatient and ready to give up, I found that there was hope for me after all.

My difficulties in t'ai chi class all came from one central problem. Like the boy in the story, I let my impatience for what I considered to be success get in the way of my actual learning. First of all, I expected to learn t'ai chi easily. Being a good student, I always think that learning any subject will come easily to me. Second, I was sure I would be the best student in the class. Because I usually am, I had come to place tremendous importance upon being best. Third, my teachers praise my work so often that I expected praise from my t'ai chi teacher, as well. I had come to think that praise, too, was very important. In fact, praise had become even more important to me then what I was learning!

My experience in t'ai chi, however, did not meet my expectations. Instead of being easy to learn, t'ai chi was very difficult for me. I was not the best in the class. I felt awkward and clumsy, while other students moved with grace and ease. Finally, I was not praised by my teacher. In fact, I was criticized by him. One day he actually yelled at me in front of the class, "You must learn to have patience and concentrate!" I felt humiliated and embarrassed. I wanted to give up right then and there.

But I did not give up. I had the determination to keep trying, in spite of my many false expectations. I thought about what my teacher had said. I tried to have more patience and concentrate harder. I practiced and practiced. Finally my teacher noticed I was making progress. But what he said was not exactly praise: "Not so bad. Now work more!"

I did work more—and more, and more. I found that the most rewarding things in life do not come easily. I had more trouble learning t'ai chi than anything else I had ever attempted, and yet I find it the most rewarding of my activities. Perhaps it is the great effort demanded by t'ai chi that makes it so rewarding. That was the first thing I learned in t'ai chi. The second was that being the best is not important. It is more important for students of any subject to know that they worked their hardest and tried their best. Finally, I improved, but my teacher never praised me. I came to understand that by not praising me, he was teaching me something even more important than t'ai chi. He was teaching me that learning itself is the true reward. But the most important thing I learned was to keep trying, even in the face of possible failure. Like the boy in the story, if a person concentrates and works hard, he or she is learning even if success is not immediately apparent. In other words, to concentration and hard work, add patience. The true reward is bound to follow.

Plug In

Before you go on to work on your own piece of writing, take a moment to go back and read over each of Felicia's previous drafts. Can you see how they get better and better? Then read over Felicia's final draft. We think it reads pretty smoothly and has the right tone (fairly formal) for a college-application essay. What do you think?

Take the writing you have been working on and prepare a final draft. Check for any mistakes, proofread it, proofread again for anything you may have missed at any stage, and then print out or retype a clean copy. What if you see one little overlooked mistake staring up at you from your gorgeous, final, clean, beautiful copy? Are you tempted to let it go? Don't do it! Fix it and print again.

Congratulations! You have now gone through every stage of the writing process. Give yourself several pats on the back; bid Felicia, Jocelyn, Ralph, and friends a fond farewell; and take a much deserved rest.

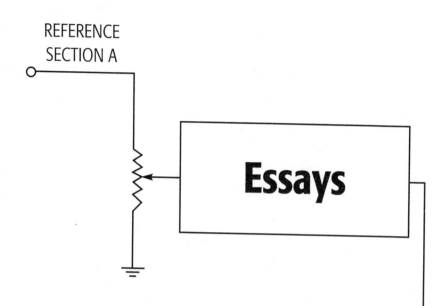

REFERENCE
SECTION A

Essays

Writing an Essay

If you have just finished going through the entire writing process in Sections One through Four, you are entering this section with your self-confidence pumped. What follows here are examples of different types of writing, with explanations and tips. There are so many different types of writing here, you should find a model for what you need. And if you don't find the model that is an exact match, you will find something close enough to get you through your particular assignment with writing power to spare.

Warming Up. Carefully review the steps in Sections One through Four. This will be the basis of your further work. Now look ahead to the examples. They may give you ideas for essays you never even thought of!

Stretching. Find the essay that you want to work on specifically. Maybe it is a review of a movie for a student newspaper. Maybe it is a memo to your boss. Look over the main headings under the essay. Familiarize yourself with it.

Working Out. Read it more carefully. Take some notes or highlight those parts of the material that seem especially important for your assignment.

Training. Refer to the Plug In sections to edit an essay we have already included for you. This will give you some practice in the particular form you're working with.

Sprint. Once you have had some practice, try writing and editing on your own. Create a rough draft of the essay you are working on. Go for it, fast. Do not stop to edit at this point. Just charge on through, getting all your ideas down on the page.

Marathon. Go through and edit your draft. Rework paragraphs. Make sure your points are supported by the necessary facts or details. Check the initial thesis statement. Is it exactly what you intend the essay to focus on? Take some quiet time to get this done.

Cooling Down. If time permits, let this essay sit for at least two days. Go back to it fresh and read again. Or give it to someone else to read. Ask them for feedback on the style, tone, facts, and power of the argument.

Personal Best. Taking into account what you have learned since your first draft, write the final draft now. Spell check it, run it off, send it on its way, and find a way to celebrate your job well done!

A QUICK REVIEW OF THE WRITING PROCESS

Remember the writing process in three steps: *think, act, repair.* These concepts are powerful tools for getting any writing job done. For your convenience, here is a brief review.

Think

Think about *your audience, your purpose,* and *your topic.* Here is a list of questions to ask yourself. Once you've answered them, you will already have a better idea of how to proceed.

> ⌁**POWER LINE**⌁
>
> The greatest possible mint of style is to make the words absolutely disappear into the thought.
>
> —Nathaniel Hawthorne

1. What tone is appropriate for your audience, formal or informal? How much do your readers know, and what do you need to tell them?
2. Why are you writing this essay anyway? To impress your teacher or an admissions committee? To communicate important information to your readers? To persuade your readers to act or think in a certain way? How can you best fulfill your purpose?

3. Have you been given a topic, or do you have to come up with one? Which topics will interest your readers most? Which will interest you? Which do you know and/or care about most? Is there a topic you are curious to know more about? Is the information you will need readily available?

Still in the thinking stage, make a plan, or outline, for your essay. This step may seem time-consuming, but it is guaranteed to save time in the end. Trust us. For your outline, don't write full sentences just notes on what you plan to include in your essay.

Act

Following your outline, write out your whole essay in complete sentences. If something in your outline does not seem to work, change it or leave it out. You wrote the outline in the first place, so you can change it if you want to. Follow these action steps:

1. Write a beginning that both draws your readers into your essay and contains your thesis statement.
2. In the body, support your thesis with details, examples, reasons, facts, explanations, anecdotes, whichever are appropriate for your topic. Make sure each supporting paragraph has just one main idea expressed in a topic sentence and that all the sentences in that paragraph support that idea.
3. Write an ending that emphasizes your main idea and leaves your readers with something to remember or think about.

Repair

Read over what you have written, revising and editing as you go along. Now that you're on the final laps of your power writing workout, stick to these steps and you'll be in great shape:

1. Cut out anything that doesn't apply to your main idea to provide the essay with unity.
2. Add anything important that you discover you have left out to give the essay completeness.

3. Change the order of sentences or even whole paragraphs if necessary to make your writing easy to follow; add transitions where needed. This will give the essay coherence.

4. Read it all again. Proofread to correct grammar, spelling, and punctuation errors and make any other improvements you think are necessary.

5. Make a clean copy. *Fini!*

Usually, people associate essays with school. "Write an essay of 250 words or more on 'My Summer Vacation,' 'My Most Unusual Experience,' 'My Trip to Pluto,'" and so on. Most high school and college courses require you to write essays. Virtually all college, grad school, and fellowship applications ask for essays. And of course, many tests, including the SAT II: Writing Test, offer questions that are answered by whole paragraphs or essays rather than short answers. (An essay that requires extensive research is also called a research report.)

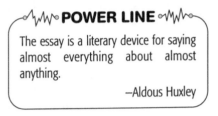

POWER LINE

The essay is a literary device for saying almost everything about almost anything.

—Aldous Huxley

If you are doing lots of writing on the job, or working with a PTA or community group, you might also find yourself writing an essay, even if you don't call it that. For example:

- Your boss asks you to write a one- to two-page summary of your department's experience with the company's new vacation policy.

- They are going to build an incinerator just a few miles from your home, and your local community group wants you to write the position paper explaining why you and your neighbors are all opposed to the plan.

- You have to write a memo explaining how to use the new photocopier.

- Good old Harry is retiring, and your company newsletter is soliciting "I Remember Harry" stories.

HOW DO YOU WRITE AN ESSAY?

A written essay is a piece of nonfiction writing. Generally, an essay should have one overall main idea, expressed in a thesis statement that usually comes in the first paragraph, or introduction. The body, or main part, of an essay should be logically divided into paragraphs, each of which has a main idea that supports the overall main idea. Each paragraph consists of sentences that support its main idea. The concluding paragraph of an essay usually summarizes or emphasizes the important points made in the body of the essay. That about sums it up!

Over years of taking "essay tests" and being assigned "essays," you may feel that this word has taken on rather mysterious, even sinister connotations. Just what is an essay, anyway? Literally, "essay" means *attempt*. That's a big help, you think. Somewhere in your foggiest distant past, some teacher has probably told you that, and it doesn't mean anything more now than it did then. So here is the accepted definition:

"An essay is a short composition which is usually in prose . . . and which discusses, either formally or informally, one or more topics."—Karl Beckson and Arthur Ganz, *A Reader's Guide to Literary Terms: A Dictionary*

Add to this that an essay is a piece of nonfiction writing (you didn't make it up) and that "short" means several paragraphs to 25 pages (if you call that brief). Oh, and the "usually in prose" bit is in there because in the 18th century, Alexander Pope wrote two famous essays in verse: "An Essay on Man" and "An Essay on Criticism." Good for him.

Other writing purposes an essay can fill:

- Explore a personal response to a person, work of art, event, or idea *(personal essay, personal response to literature)*
- Persuade readers to share your opinion and perhaps to take a particular action *(persuasive essay)*
- Explain how to do something or show how something works *(how-to essay/process analysis)*
- Compare and contrast two or more ideas, events, works of literature, or other things *(compare-and-contrast essay, comparative analysis)*

 191

- Show how certain causes result in a particular effect *(cause-and-effect essay)*
- Describe a problem and offer a solution *(problem-and-solution essay)*

An Essay Should Be Unified

The main idea of an essay is stated, usually near the beginning, in one or more sentences called the *thesis statement.*

- Every single paragraph should support the thesis statement.
- Every single sentence in every paragraph should support the main idea of the paragraph.
- Every single word in every sentence should relate to the main idea of the sentence.

An essay in which all three of these requirements is met is called a *unified essay,* or an essay that has *unity.* Some ways to "support" an idea are by:

- Giving a reason
- Giving an example
- Giving a personal response
- Offering descriptive details

An Essay Should Be Complete

While a good essay should contain no irrelevant information, it needs to contain all the relevant information readers will need to follow the writer's ideas. Background information about your topic, details, reasons, examples, and explanations are some of the types of information that should be included.

An Essay Should Be Coherent

The paragraphs and sentences in your essay should be in the best possible order: one that makes sense, is logical, and helps the reader follow your ideas. If you are writing a persuasive essay, offering (hopefully!) persuasive arguments to your readers, make sure that all the sentences that relate to one particular argument go together. If you are describing a place, choose a logical order for the details, such as from near to far, or from far to near.

If you are writing about particular people, explain who they are *when you introduce them,* not several paragraphs later. Likewise, if you are introducing a word or phrase that needs defining, give the definition as close as possible to the word. Transitional words and phrases, such as *for example, on the other hand, next, however, and therefore,* help make an essay coherent by letting the reader see how a sentence is related or connected to the prior one.

A good way to make sure your essay is coherent is to picture a reader who knows absolutely nothing about the topic. Then ask yourself, "What does my reader need to know first? Then what? What after that?"

Write a Good Essay. Instructions for a good essay:

1. A good essay should be unified. Translation: Nothing irrelevant, no padding, no fluff.

2. A good essay should be coherent. Translation: Nothing that seems out of place, nothing confusing.

3. A good essay is well-written. Translation: Varied sentences, good word choice, no mistakes. Easy as 1, 2, 3! (Well, almost!)

An Essay May Be Formal or Informal

Depending on your audience and purpose, you may write in a *formal tone,* meaning no contractions or slangy expressions, not using the words *you* and *I,* and writing in the third person only (*"One* can see thus and so," etcetera).

If your essay is meant to be *informal* (like the writing style in this book, for example), those rules loosen up quite a bit, but your grammar, spelling, and punctuation should still be carefully checked.

POWER LINE

When audiences come to see us authors lecture it is largely in the hope that we'll be funnier to look at than to read.

—Sinclair Lewis

THE FORMULA FOR SUCCESS

Many writers, both experienced and otherwise, experience serious sinking-of-the-heart spells when they are faced with an essay assignment, but don't you succumb. We are about to give you a secret *Writing Power* formula that works every time.

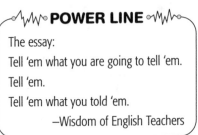

POWER LINE

The essay:
Tell 'em what you are going to tell 'em.
Tell 'em.
Tell 'em what you told 'em.
—Wisdom of English Teachers

Introduction. Introduce the point you want to make, or in writer-ese, write your thesis statement. If you are writing about a person who influenced you, tell who the person is and suggest what was important about him or her. If you are taking a position on an issue, name the issue, give your opinion, and suggest why you care. Then, in one or a few sentences, give a little preview of how you plan to support your thesis statement in the body of your essay.

Body. This is the main part of your essay. Make three points, one paragraph per point, to support your main idea. Your three points might be examples, arguments, reasons, or incidents. If you are describing an important event, break down the event into three parts. If you are telling about an important person, give three examples of why he or she is important to you. If you're making an argument, give three reasons why readers should agree with you.

Why the magic number three? No particular reason, but two doesn't seem like enough, and more than three might make your essay too long. The "Rule of Three" is not really a rule. You don't have to stick to it rigidly, but it's a good guide.

Conclusion. Here you drive your point home. You might restate your thesis statement, using different words. You might summarize your main points, explaining how they support your main idea. Or you could end with a question, an image, an anecdote, or any other device that will linger in your audience's mind and keep readers thinking about your ideas.

One thing you should *not* do however, is introduce any new ideas or issues that you will not be supporting or explaining. That only leaves your readers confused and unsatisfied.

CHAPTER NINETEEN

The Personal Essay

A personal essay, as you know by now, focuses on an incident or person from your own life. Felicia, back in Section Two, was writing a personal essay for her college application. If you want an in-depth lesson in personal essay writing, go back and follow Felicia's progress step by step. Here, you'll find the quick-and-easy version.

STEP ONE: THINK

Since whoever is giving you this assignment does not know too much about your personal life, the assignment is likely to be fairly general: It's up to you to find a topic.

Focus Your Personal Essay. Here are some questions that can help you focus your thoughts. You might jot down the answers quickly, without thinking too much, on a separate piece of paper:

- If my best friend were asked about my four best qualities, what would he or she say? What examples would my friend give?
- If my favorite teacher were asked about my four best qualities, what would he or she say? What examples would my teacher give?
- What would I most like to change about myself? Why?
- What challenges me?

Use your responses as your guide to choosing a topic that will interest both your audience (probably your teacher or a college admissions committee) and yourself.

Once you've found your topic, develop your ideas before you start to write. Depending on your topic, brainstorming, focused freewriting, or a word web might be good techniques to use.

Next, write your thesis statement; that is, clearly state your main idea in one or two sentences.

When you are ready to organize your ideas, you might want to use an analysis frame, as Felicia did. Write down your main points and list details under each one.

Think about the order of your ideas and experiment with different orders. You will probably be using *chronological order* if you are telling about an event in your life, *order of importance* if you are telling about an important person in your life, and *order of impression* or *spatial order* if you are describing a person or place. You may want to use more than one type of order if you are, for example, describing a person's appearance in one paragraph (order of impression or spatial order) and explaining the person's place in your life in another (order of importance). You may feel ready to write at this point, or you might feel more confident working from a formal outline.

STEP TWO: ACT

Using your outline or other development notes, begin your first draft, remembering that anything you write now may be changed later. Then follow our handy workflow order:

- Concentrate first on writing strong opening sentences, stating your main idea, asking a question, or telling an anecdote.
- In the body, or main part, of your essay, sensory details, concrete examples, memories, and anecdotes can add interest, depending on your specific topic, of course. Each paragraph should contain a topic sentence that states its main idea.

- For your conclusion, you might try leaving the reader with a strong impression or visual image to remember. Another way to go is to tell an anecdote, but remember that too many of these can become tiresome. If you choose to begin and end with a story, fine, but don't include anecdotes in the main part of your essay.

STEP THREE: REPAIR

Cut out anything you've written that is irrelevant to your main idea. Be ruthless—even if you have written a fabulous description of your grandmother's charming parlor, if it has nothing to do with what you learned about courage from your grandmother, cut it out. (You can keep it in your clippings file for another essay on what you learned from your grandmother about interior decorating.)

Next, add any information you've left out. If your essay needs livening up, try adding sensory details, vivid language, or additional facts that might bring your subject to life for your readers. For coherence, check that you have used the type of order most appropriate for your subject matter.

And of course, proofread for grammar, spelling, punctuation, and any other errors you may have made. Check, especially, for too much repetition. In a personal essay there is a temptation to begin too many sentences with the word *I.* Try varying your sentence beginnings to eliminate repetition. Use the following checklist on this page to make sure you haven't missed anything in the "repair" phase of your essay.

Personal Essay Checklist. Give your personal essay the old mental spit and polish. Does it pass high standards? Find out with our handy checklist:

- Will the beginning of my essay capture readers' interest?
- Do I state my main idea clearly?
- Do I support my main idea with sufficient concrete examples, sensory details, and interesting facts?
- Have I cut out any irrelevant information?
- Do I use lively, vivid language?

- Are my sentences varied to avoid repetition, especially repetition of the word *I* ?
- Does my conclusion leave readers with a lasting impression?

Plug In

Here is the first draft of the personal essay that Patrice wrote for a school assignment. Try repairing the essay by using proofreader marks to edit the essay directly on the draft (or on a separate sheet of paper). Compare your repair to our final draft.

A Day I Will Never Forget

It used to be that students joined in strikes and antiwar protests. Nowadays, all young people do is watch MTV or shop at the mall. I was exactly the same was everybody else I really was no different. I was completely ignorant of current events. I never read a paper, watched the news, read a news magazine, looked at a documentary, or did anything to educate myself about current events. I did know all about the personal lives of popular TV stars. And movie stars.

In my social studies class, we had an assignment to interview an older person who had lived a long time. We were supposed to ask that person about the changes he or she had witnessed in his or her lifetime. I decided to interview my neighbor, Mrs. Fletcher. She had never spoken to me much before. She would not have much to say! I could just go ahead and finish the assignment quickly. Then I would be done with this stupid project. Or so I thought.

But Mrs. Fletcher started telling me about the time before the civil rights movement. There was a lot I did not know. In the 1950s, African

Americans did not have any of the same rights that they do now. They did not have any of the same rights as white people. They had completely different lives. Mrs. Fletcher talked about what she and other people did. I became filled with shame at my own ignorance of everything I did not know. I did not know how I could have been so unaware.

From that moment on, politics and history became my favorite subjects. I began to talk to grown-ups about their memories of earlier times in the past. I tried to learn about the hot topics of our own time today. I helped a local candidate.

In school they tried to tell us that there was no society freer than the United States, but that was only part of the story. By reading about the events of the past, I learned that freedom is not something you are given. It is something you have to fight for. And when you do, you have to make sure no one tries to take it away again.

Plug In Solution

Here is our final draft of the personal essay. So how does it compare to what you would have done?

A Day I Will Never Forget

People often complain that our generation is politically apathetic. Just 25 years ago, it was common for students to join in strikes and antiwar protests, but nowadays, the stereotype goes, young people are more likely to be found watching MTV or shopping at the mall. I certainly was no different. Appallingly ignorant of current events, I never read a paper or watched the news, but I knew all about the personal lives of popular TV and movie stars. Then something happened to change my outlook forever.

In my social studies class, we had an assignment to interview an older person about the changes he or she had witnessed in his or her lifetime. I decided to interview my neighbor, Mrs. Fletcher. Since she had never spoken to me much before, I figured she would have little to say and I could complete the assignment quickly.

To my surprise, Mrs. Fletcher started telling me about a world I had never known: life in our town before the civil rights movement. I was astonished to learn that in the 1950s, African Americans went to separate schools, rode at the backs of buses, and were prevented from living in white neighborhoods. As Mrs. Fletcher talked about how she and other African Americans helped break the color barrier by insisting on being served at white-only lunch counters, I became filled with shame at my own ignorance. How could I have been so unaware?

From that moment on, politics and history became my passions. I began to talk to my parents, my teachers, and other adults about their memories of earlier times. I started reading the newspaper, especially the editorial page, trying to learn about the burning issues of our own time. I even volunteered to stuff envelopes for a local candidate who I thought might make our own community a better place.

In school we had been taught that there was no society freer than the United States, but that was only part of the story. By reading about the political struggles of minorities, women, blue-collar workers and others, I learned that freedom is not something you are given. It is something you have to fight for. And once you win it, you have to make sure no one tries to take it away again. That is why I will never forget the day I interviewed Mrs. Fletcher. It is the day I became politically aware.

Plug In Again

Now it's your turn. Use the stages of Thinking, Acting, and Repairing to write your own personal essay about a day you'll never forget, a related personal essay topic, or a subject you've actually been assigned.

WRITING A COLLEGE APPLICATION ESSAY

Most colleges, grad schools, and fellowship committees will ask you to write "something about yourself," usually in 250 to 500 words (one or two typed, double-spaced pages). Sometimes you will be asked to choose your own topic. Sometimes you will receive a specific assignment to write about a person who influenced you, a key event in your life, or a particular issue that interests you. As your face your writing task, ask questions.

1. Who is your audience? A committee.
2. What is your purpose? You have three. One is to impress the committee with your writing skills. The second is to convince the committee that you are an interesting person who will enhance the college community both intellectually and socially. The third is to communicate ideas about your topic.

Let's take the committee members first. You will want to write an essay that is not too long, because they have read so many that they will be getting sick of them. You'll want to write in a formal style and not make any sloppy mistakes. Write on a topic that may actually interest members of the committee. And on the topic of topics, you will want to choose one that shows an interesting side of your personality or that highlights your personal strengths that cannot be measured by grades and test scores.

For example, Felicia's essay about what she learned from studying t'ai chi introduces Felicia as a person who has the initiative to try out new things and is interested in personal growth. If a specific topic doesn't come to mind after just a few minutes of nail-biting and brain-wracking, go back and read chapter 5, Finding a Topic. You'll find step-by-step information on how to find a topic quickly before your application is due.

WRITING A TEST ESSAY

Writing for any test is a special case because you have a time limit and you are not at home in your favorite chair with a cup of coffee and a snack within arm's reach. Thinking about your essay even before you see the test can pave the way for an easier time on Test Day. We've broken down the mechanics of essay writing for tests into easy-to-digest components.

The Length of Your Essay. Let's say you're taking the SAT II: Writing Test. Your essay may be somewhat shorter than a college application essay, but probably not much shorter. The SAT essays that get the best scores tend to be from three to five paragraphs long (five paragraphs = Introduction + three "body" paragraphs + Conclusion), and those paragraphs contain more than one or two sentences each. In other words, on Test Day, fill up as many lines on the answer sheet as possible, but do not fill up lines just for the sake of sounding "important." A short, but complete, clear essay in which every sentence is related to the main idea is better than a long, rambling essay that is full of padding and fluff. Remember that unity, completeness, and coherence are your friends.

Your Audience and Purpose. If you think about your audience and purpose now, you won't have to waste time on T-Day. Who is your audience? Probably high school teachers and college professors. What is your purpose? To show them that you know how to write well and think logically, of course; but also, to show that you have read a few books and that you know something about the world. So refer to current events, history, or literature in your essay, if at all possible.

For example, let's say you love the novels of Jane Austen, and you are asked to respond to the statement, "The strong do what they wish. Agree or Disagree." You might give one example based on your own life, and two examples based on Jane Austen's characters. Or, if you know a lot about World War II, your examples of strong people's actions might relate to the careers of Hitler, Mussolini, Churchill, and Roosevelt. If you think this is showing off, it is! But so what? Part of your purpose is to "show your stuff."

Use the Writing Process. Yes, even for the 20 minutes you get to write your essay. Here's how to divide up your time:

- *Think.* On scrap paper, make an outline or use some other prewriting technique to get your thoughts in order. This step should take you about five minutes.

- *Act.* Write a good, solid, three to five paragraphs, starting with an introduction, proceeding to three supporting paragraphs, and ending with a strong conclusion. Be as correct as possible, because you won't have much time for repair work. Allow about 13 minutes for this step.

- *Repair.* Change a few words if necessary, maybe add a sentence or two. Then proofread your work, correcting any grammar or spelling errors. You should leave yourself about two minutes for this step.

Why You'll Need No. 2 Pencils. Finally, we hardly need remind you to be neat. Just think of your audience. Each reader of the SAT Writing Test is reading dozens, perhaps hundreds of essays. Have sympathy for that person's tired eyes, and make your work as easy to read as possible. While we're on that subject, bring No. 2 pencils with good erasers so you will be able to make neat revisions and corrections.

CHAPTER TWENTY

The Persuasive Essay

A persuasive essay is one in which the writer tries to persuade readers to share an opinion and perhaps to take a particular action as a result.

To write a persuasive essay, as with all types of writing, you can't go wrong if you use your secret weapon (the writing process) and the no-longer-secret formula for writing an essay.

STEP ONE: THINK

Your writing may be motivated by an opinion about which you feel strongly. On an exam, you may be presented with an opinion and asked to respond to it in different ways. Or you may be completing a college application or school assignment that asks you to express your opinion on a topic of your choice. If you keep a journal or a clippings file, those are excellent places to look for opinions that you have formed. If not, freewriting will help you focus on an issue about which you feel strongly. In any case, your opinion will be your thesis statement. Here are several examples:

- TV is a bad influence on children.
- Our company should increase vacation time from one to two weeks.
- The legal age of maturity should be lowered from 21 to 18.
- Fathers and mothers should take equal responsibility for child care.
- Cigarettes should be declared illegal.
- Smokers should not be discriminated against.

You may want to do some reading and note taking on your topic. That will serve the double purpose of giving you ideas for the arguments and reasons for your opinion, and may also provide you with facts and statistics, effective ammunition in a persuasive essay. Use brainstorming techniques to make a list including every reason for your opinion that you can think of. Then choose the ones (at least three, if possible) you think you'll be able to develop best.

Organize Your Persuasive Essay Ideas. An analysis frame (see chapter 9) works particularly well for organizing ideas for a persuasive essay. Write your thesis statement at the top of a blank page; then list the major reasons you will use to support your opinion. Those reasons will be the topics of each of your main paragraphs. Finally, list supporting details such as facts, statistics, and logical arguments under your reasons.

Put Your Ideas in Order

Your next job is to put your ideas in order. The preferred order for a persuasive essay is order of importance. Experiment to see which you prefer least to most important, or most to least important. Each option has its advantages. The former lets you save your most convincing arguments for last, and readers sometimes best remember the last things they read. The latter gives you the advantage of "coming on strong."

Jot your reasons down in different orders to see which works best for you. At this point, you may decide you do not have to make a formal outline, because your revised analysis frame will do the same job. Just add what you plan to write in your introduction and conclusion. On the other hand, by making an outline you may get additional ideas, because the more you think about a topic the more ideas come to mind. It's up to you.

STEP TWO: ACT

Whether you opt for a quick, loose draft or a tight one, remember that your essay will have to end up with air-tight arguments and iron-clad logic. If, while drafting, you see that a certain argument doesn't really work, you will have to scrap them and find new ones.

Either way, start off with an introduction that grabs your audience's attention and presents your thesis. Write one paragraph per reason, naming the reason and then adding facts and examples to back it up. Finally, conclude with a paragraph that restates your thesis and shows why this is an important issue.

STEP THREE: REPAIR

When you edit a persuasive essay, pay particular attention to the way your arguments unfold. An argument that is irrelevant or has holes in it is worse than none at all. Take it out or revise it so that it "holds water." You should also make sure that you have included any information or explanations that your audience needs to understand your reasoning.

Give your essay a whole reading devoted to checking transitions. Transitional words and phrases such as *however, therefore, in the first place,* and *most importantly* are essential to a coherent persuasive essay.

Persuasive Essay Checklist. When you edit and revise a personal essay, follow this handy roster of considerations:

- Have I clearly stated my opinion in my introductory paragraph?
- Are my reasons in order of importance?
- Have I chosen the strongest possible facts and examples to support my reasons?
- Do all my arguments "hold water"?
- Have I taken opposing views into account?
- Have I used transitions effectively?
- Have I included all the information my reader needs to understand and accept my reasons?
- Does my concluding paragraph restate my opinion and highlight the issue my essay discusses?

Plug In

Blake had to write a persuasive essay for a college application. Here is his draft, followed by our suggested final draft. Edit his first draft (either in the book or on your own paper), then compare your work and your reasoning with ours.

Directions: Please write an essay on a topic you feel strongly about in the space provided.

I think the age of maturity ought to be lowered to 18. Obviously, 21 is a number they just pulled out of a hat. What about the 18-year-olds who have to be responsible? People in the Army. Kids with jobs, full-time jobs. Some people even get married or harder still, have children.

The true test of maturity is being able to accept responsibility for your actions. What if you commit a crime, have money, hire a super lawyer, and then get off completely free? And then go on television and write a book and make money. That is not mature. Just being over 21 does not make that mature.

Many teenagers do accept responsibility for their actions. Teenagers may be even more responsible than adults. For example, teenagers do not cause as many drunk-driving accidents as adults do.

Some people do not agree. They say that many teenagers are not mature. What about all the teenage pregnancies? What about the drug users? What about the teens who commit crimes? But people over 21 also act irresponsibly. The solution is not to blame one particular age group, but rather, to make everyone be responsible for their actions, legally and morally responsible.

In conclusion, more and more teenagers are facing adult responsibilities. We need a law to recognize that fact.

Plug In Solution

Okay, here is our revised draft. Compare it to yours. Any differences? Why?

Currently, the United States recognizes that a person "matures" when he or she reaches the legal age of 21, but I think the age of maturity ought to be lowered to 18 instead. Certainly, we can all agree that 21 is an arbitrary number. Many 18-year-olds are in positions where they must act responsibly: they enlist in the Armed Forces, work full time, marry, and even raise children. Shouldn't we recognize their adult responsibilities with a law that says they are adults?

The true test of maturity is being able to accept responsibility for one's actions. In our society, people who commit crimes, but have enough money, hire the best lawyers and get acquitted. Then they go on television or write books about their "ordeal," and make even more money. Are they mature? Are they any more mature for being over the age of 21?

Many teenagers, on the other hand, do accept responsibility for their actions. As a group, teenagers may behave even more responsibly than many adults. For example, in 1993, according to the National Highway Traffic Safety Administration, only 7.6 percent of those aged 16 to 20 were involved in fatal alcohol-related traffic crashes, as compared to 14.1 percent of those aged 21 to 24 and 10.1 percent of those aged 25 to 34.

Some might argue that many teenagers are not mature. They would point to the numbers of teenage unwed pregnancies, to teenage drug use, and to teen crime as examples of the ways in which people under 21 have difficulty handling adult responsibilities. But people over 21 also act irresponsibly with regard to sex, drugs, and crime. The solution is not to blame one particular age group, but rather, to hold everyone accountable, legally and morally.

The fact is that more and more teenagers are facing adult responsibilities at work, in the Armed Forces, in marriage, and in their roles as parents. A law that recognized that fact would help people of all ages behave maturely and responsibly.

 209

Plug In Again

Now write your own 250 to 500 word persuasive essay on a topic of your choosing, or take your own position on whether the age of maturity should be lowered from 21 to 18. Use the checklist as you revise and edit.

CHAPTER TWENTY-ONE

The Process Analysis (How To) Essay

A process analysis essay is sometimes known as a "how-to essay," because it tells you *how* to do something. We prefer *process analysis*, however, because this type of essay can also explain how a process happens or how something works. Here are some examples:

- Your co-workers *still* don't know how to use the coffee machine, and you have to write them another memo!

- Your premed teacher wants you to prove that you really do understand why fat in the diet is bad for the heart.

- Your family can't seem to make sense of the manual for the new VCR, so you are writing them a simple set of instructions on how to program it.

- You are writing promotional material for investors who might want to finance your company's new video-editing system. In order to put up the money, they want to know how the system works.

As always, the writing process is your best friend. However, you may have to slightly alter the secret formula for an essay. Because your process may have any number of major steps, the Rule of Three will probably not apply here. Begin a new paragraph for each major step you are describing.

STEP ONE: THINK

Start by making a list of steps in chronological order. For a more complex process, you might also use a flow chart, showing how steps in the process are interrelated. Here are Jeannie's notes on costume design for her theater class:

How a Costume Designer Prepares for a Show

1. Research and preparation

2. Sketches

3. Rehearsals

4. Build costumes

5. Fittings

6. Last-minute changes

These are the *major steps* in the process. Now break down each step into simple actions. Be as detailed as possible better too much than too little at this point. If it turns out that you have gone overboard, you can cut back in the drafting or revising stage. Break it down now:

How a Costume Designer Prepares for a Show

1. Research and preparation

   a. reads play

   b. meets with director, discusses ideas

   c. does research (looks at historical material from the period and country where the play takes place, looks at what other designers have done for the same play)

2. Sketches draws colored pictures that show each character in costume

   (NOTE: If a character changes costume, that means two sketches!)

3. Rehearsals watches actors, talks to director, gets more ideas

4. Builds costumes

    a. chooses fabrics and trimmings

    b. measures actors

    c. cuts out and sews costumes

5. Fittings

    a. actors try on clothes

    b. adjustments made so clothes will fit

6. Last-minute changes; examples:

    a. an actress has trouble walking in a long skirt—maybe shorten skirt?

    b. an actor looks a little drab, even though the sketch looked okay—maybe give him a big feather for his hat, or a shiny sash?

STEP TWO: ACT

Start with an introduction that makes clear what you're writing about and why. Is your purpose to demonstrate your knowledge (as on a test), to teach your audience how to do something, or to give your audience an appreciation for a fascinating or important process?

In the body of your work, use transition words to show the relationships between steps. Remember, you are explaining each step in chronological order, so time-order transition words are especially useful:

first	then	until
second	afterwards	finally
third	later	earlier
next	before	

Don't forget to define any unfamiliar words or concepts. You may need a long explanation or just a few words in parentheses. Here's how Jeannie did it:

> . . . Then the costume designer does research. That is, he or she looks through a variety of books, magazines, photographs, and paintings to get ideas for what the clothes of the period might look like. The designer might also view movies that are set in the same period.

> . . . The next step is to make costume sketches, or colored drawings of the clothes that each actor will wear.

> . . . Finally, the designer makes an appointment with each actor for a fitting. The actor tries on the costume so that the designer can make alterations.

Your conclusion should either tell the results of the process or the benefits of knowing how to perform it. If you are writing about how fat affects the heart, for example, you might end by saying:

> As a result, the heart is overworked every time it beats, a condition that might result in heart disease.

The instructions for the VCR can be less formal, since the audience is your own family:

> So now you'll never again be torn between going out to dinner and watching the NCAA basketball finals. With this dandy set of instructions in hand, you can do both!

STEP THREE: REPAIR

Check to make sure you have given the steps in the clearest possible order. Double-check to make sure you have used transitions effectively, explained unfamiliar terms, and mentioned the results or benefits of the process. Use the following checklist as a guide.

Process Analysis Essay Checklist. When you edit and revise a process analysis, just follow the yellow brick list:

- Have I clearly introduced the process I am explaining?
- Have I included every step in the correct order?
- Have I used transition words to show chronological order?
- Have I defined all terms that may be unfamiliar to readers?
- Does my conclusion make clear the results or benefits of the process?
- When I read my work aloud, does my explanation sound clear and easy to understand?

One final suggestion: Find someone who knows nothing about the process you're describing. Have him or her read your essay. Can this person now explain the process to *you?* If not, what do you need to clarify?

Plug In

Here is the process analysis Jeannie wrote. Edit Jeannie's rough draft, keeping an eye out for undefined terms and steps presented in a confusing order. Do your edit here or, better yet, use a separate sheet of paper. Then compare your edits to ours in our suggested final draft.

From Concept to Clothing: How a Costume Designer Designs a Show

Audiences sitting in a darkened theater may be awed at the beautiful costumes but did you ever wondered how they got that way?

First the costume designer reads the play. Then he or she meets with the director and discusses ideas. Somewhere in here, the designer also does research.

Sketches are very important. They show what the costume will look like. Usually, they also tell what material will be used, so everyone can picture exactly how the costume will be.

 215

Of course, the designer has to go to rehearsals! And it is very important for him or her to meet with the actors. When the costumes are ready, the actors have to go to fittings. The designer adjusts the clothes if they do not fit. Too tight, too long, weird color, just does not look right.

Then, the designer actually has to make the clothes. Naturally, he or she has to measure the actors! The choice of fabric is very important. Imagine the difference between a skirt made out of rich, dark velvet, and one made out of heavy gray flannel. You would get a totally different image of the character.

Sometimes there are last minute changes. Say an actress is playing a very glamorous character in a long skirt. But she keeps tripping on the skirt. She would need a hem! Or if an actor looks a little drab even if the sketch looked OK a designer might add a big feather for his hat or a shiny sash.

Plug In Solution

Voila! Here's Jeannie's final draft. What do you think of it?

From Concept to Clothing: How a Costume Designer Designs a Show

When you are sitting in a darkened theater, you may be awed at the beautiful costumes, but have you ever wondered how they got that way? A costume designer has created every piece of clothing that the actors wear, through a long, slow, and fascinating process.

First the costume designer reads the play. Then he or she does research. That is, he or she looks through a variety of books, magazines, photographs, paintings, and other materials to get ideas for what the clothes might look like. Finally, he or she meets with the director and discusses ideas. Since costumes can help set the mood of a play, the director's input is very important.

Now it is time to make costume sketches—colored drawings of the clothes that each character will wear. Usually, they also tell what material will be used, so everyone can picture exactly how the costume will be. Imagine the difference between a skirt made out of rich, dark velvet, and one made out of heavy gray flannel. Each choice gives you a totally different image of the character.

Most of the time, the sketches are finished before rehearsals begin. But the designer usually goes to at least some rehearsals to get a feeling for the actors' personalities. Perhaps the designer imagined a character as quiet and shy, whereas the actor is playing that character as loud and flamboyant. The designer might need to change the costume sketch.

Then the designer actually has to measure the actor and make the clothes. Finally, it is time for fittings (trying the clothes on the actors). The designer adjusts the clothes if they do not fit, are uncomfortable, or just do not look quite right.

Sometimes a designer must make last-minute changes. Perhaps an actress is having trouble with a long skirt, or an actor's costume seems a little drab. The designer might shorten the actress's skirt and give the actor a big feather for his hat.

The designer's job can be long and difficult. But it is all worthwhile on opening night, when every actor is wearing the perfect costume for his or her character!

Plug In Again

Now write your own how-to essay or process analysis. Think of a task you'd like to teach or a process you'd like to explain. Write a brief essay, and try it out on a reader who might be interested. Can your reader explain the process back to you?

CHAPTER TWENTY-TWO

The Comparison-and-Contrast Essay

To *compare* is to point out similarities between two item, and to *contrast* is to point out differences. A comparison-and-contrast essay, therefore, tells how two or more items are similar and how they are different. You might compare and

contrast books, health insurance coverage, applicants for a job, candidates for political office, plans to improve a school, historical figures, or any other people, places, things, or ideas that you can think of.

As you might imagine from the preceding list, a compare-and-contrast ("c-and-c," for short) essay might have one of many purposes. Most obviously, it can be used to evaluate or to demonstrate which of the alternatives is a better choice than the other. On the other hand, your purpose in a c-and-c essay might simply be to inform. If you are comparing and contrasting Richard Nixon and Ronald Reagan for a history paper, for example, you aren't necessarily supposed to pick your favorite president. Instead, by discussing the two men together, you might learn new things about each one. Both their similarities and their differences might surprise you and your readers.

Okay, back to the writing process!

STEP ONE: THINK

You may already know which two (or more) items you need to compare. If you have been assigned this type of essay and have to choose your own topic, choose carefully. If the items you pick are too similar or too different, there won't be any point in comparing or contrasting them.

A useful way to begin a c-and-c essay is to make a Venn diagram or a compare-and-contrast chart. You can find samples of these back in chapter 9, Organizing Your Ideas. You can also prepare by answering questions like the following:

- What are the most important aspects of each item?
- Which of these important qualities do the two items share?
- Which important qualities belong to one item but not the other?
- Which similarities surprise me?
- Which differences surprise me?
- How will my comparison and contrast of these two items change my readers' views? What conclusions might they draw?

Before you go any further, think about your *overall purpose.*

- Will you be making the point that there isn't really much to choose between the two items because one is as good as the other?
- Will you be demonstrating that one item is preferable?
- Will readers find that the differences between the two items are more important than the similarities, or vice versa?

In one or two sentences, write the answer to one of the above questions. What you have written will be your thesis statement.

One more thing before you act. For a c-and-c essay, we strongly recommend drafting a formal outline. Organization is so important that you should give yourself a chance to see how your whole essay will be laid out before you begin to write. An outline will save you time on the repair end.

STEP TWO: ACT

Your introduction will serve three purposes:

- Naming the two items to be considered in the essay
- Getting your readers' attention by explaining why your comparisons and contrasts will be interesting or useful to them
- Announcing your main idea in your thesis statement

Nadine interviewed several applicants for a job as art director in her company's advertising department. The choice has been narrowed down to two candidates, and Nadine is writing a memo to her boss comparing and contrasting the two applicants. Here is her introductory paragraph:

> We are in the fortunate position of having two excellent applicants for the position of art director. At first glance, Bart Samson and Homer Swanson seem to be equally well-qualified. However, after a closer look, I believe Bart is the far stronger candidate.

When you come to write the body of your c-and-c essay, you have two choices. You could *describe the main aspects of the first item and then the main aspects of the second*. Nadine could have written the following topic sentence for her first body paragraph:

> Bart Samson is creative, enterprising, and highly individual. Each of the five ad campaigns he worked on at his last job were innovative, even ground-breaking. Homer Swanson, on the other hand, has produced good, competent work, but has not shown himself to be an inventive or innovative thinker.

Another way to go is to *compare and contrast the two items feature by feature*, pointing out the similarities and differences as you go. Nadine chose this option:

> Both Bart and Homer have worked for prestigious advertising agencies. Both have good references. Each has several successful campaigns to his credit. However, Bart's campaigns tend to be unusual and innovative with a sense of humor, whereas Homer's work is more conventional and perhaps a little dull.

Whichever choice you make, you will have to provide concrete examples to illustrate each major point you make. If possible, make at least three main points with one paragraph for each. After claiming that Bart is more creative and giving specific examples to prove that (first main point), Nadine could go on to show that while Homer has a better work attendance record (second main point) and is a better illustrator (third main point), creativity is the most important quality the company is looking for (conclusion).

Your conclusion should help your readers draw conclusions. What insights have you gained from comparing and contrasting? Nadine's conclusion was that her company should hire Bart, the more creative candidate. (If she worked for a more traditional agency, she might have chosen Homer.)

STEP THREE: REPAIR

Transition words are especially useful in a c-and-c essay, because they help the reader keep track of the points you are making. Here are some you might want to add in your Stage One revision:

To Point Out Similarities

like, likewise, similarly, in the same way, also, as, just as, both, moreover, furthermore, in addition, besides, along with

To Point Out Differences

unlike, on the other hand, in contrast with, by contrast, however, but, instead, rather than, whereas

In revisions done during Stage Two, check your organization. If you started off comparing your two items feature by feature, make sure you've used that plan consistently throughout the body of your essay. If you switch from one type of organization to another, your readers will be confused and miss your point (or give up reading entirely).

In Stage Three revision, look at your word choices and, if necessary, substitute concrete, specific words for vague, general ones. For example, if you've used the word "better" repeatedly, look for words or phrases that answer the question, "Better in which way?" Here are some possibilities, depending on your topic, of course: stronger, more assertive, better-experienced, more reliable, more charismatic, a better "team player."

Our much-in-demand checklist will help you remember all of the above when you edit and revise a comparison-and-contrast (better known as a c-and-c) essay.

Comparison-and-Contrast Essay Checklist. When you edit and revise a c-and-c, follow these considerations:

- Does my introduction let readers know why they should be interested in reading my essay?
- Does my introduction name the items I am comparing and contrasting?
- Does my introduction make my purpose clear with a well-written thesis statement?
- Have I organized my arguments consistently, either item by item or feature by feature?
- Does my conclusion help readers draw their own conclusions about what to think or do?
- Have I used transitions to point out similarities and differences?
- Have I provided enough examples to illustrate my points?
- Have I used concrete, specific language?

Plug In

Otis was taking a music-appreciation course. He wrote the following essay comparing and contrasting gospel music and the blues. Edit his rough draft (in the book or on your own paper), then take a look at our final draft. Watch out for:

- Places to add transition words
- Missing definitions or explanations
- Places where examples could make an item come to life
- Missing parts of an overview or conclusion

Have you ever gone out on Saturday night to hear someone sing the blues? Have you ever gone to a Baptist church the next morning and heard a joyful gospel song? Both are great music!

When you first hear gospel music and the blues, you can't help noticing how different they are in mood and in the stories they tell. Blues songs are sad, full of heartbreak and disappointment. Gospel songs are the happiest songs you'll ever hear, full of joy and hope.

They both have African roots and similar African musical forms. For example, blues is known for its "blue" or "bent" notes. Gospel music has bent notes. In gospel music, the preacher calls out a line and the congregation answers. A blues singer sings a line, and an instrument echoes or answers him.

Blues and gospel music helped create what we know as rock music today. In the 1940s, black musicians in the South and in northern cities like Chicago, where black Americans had migrated in large numbers, started playing "rhythm and blues." Black artists like Ray Charles and James Brown added gospel harmonies and piano riffs to the rhythm-and-blues mix. This new sound found a wider and wider audience and came to be called "rock and roll."

So you see, gospel and blues songs have different moods and tell different kinds of stories, and their roots and musical characteristics are very similar. Many important black musicians grew up singing the blues on Saturday night and gospel songs on Sunday morning.

Plug In Solution

Not a bad draft, but here's the masterpiece, the final draft of Otis's c-and-c essay.

Have you ever gone out on Saturday night to hear someone sing the blues? Have you ever gone to a Baptist church the next morning and heard a joyful gospel song? You may think the two musical expressions have nothing in common, but if you listen closely and study their histories, you will find some surprising similarities.

When you first hear gospel music and the blues, you can't help noticing how different they are in mood and in the stories they tell. Blues songs are sad, full of heartbreak and disappointment. They talk about everyday problems like losing a job or a girlfriend (or boyfriend), like having no money or no friends. Gospel songs, on the other hand, are the happiest songs you'll ever hear, full of joy and hope. Unlike the blues, gospel songs tell about the power of faith in tunes so catchy, they make you want to get up and dance.

Both kinds of music, however, have African roots and similar African musical forms. For example, blues is known for its "blue" or "bent" notes notes that exist somewhere in between the formal notes of the do-re-mi scale. Gospel music also has bent notes. The other characteristic of African music they both have is a call-and-response pattern. In gospel music, the preacher calls out a line and the congregation answers. In the same way, a blues singer intones a line, and an instrument echoes or answers him or her.

Both blues and gospel music helped create what we know as rock music today. In the 1940s, black musicians in the South and in northern cities like Chicago, where black Americans had migrated in large numbers, started playing a new type of blues that was faster and had a heavier beat. The style was called "rhythm and blues." Later, black artists like Ray Charles and James Brown added gospel harmonies and piano riffs to the rhythm-and-blues mix. This new sound found a wider and wider audience and came to be called "rock and roll."

So you see, even though gospel and blues songs have different moods and tell different kinds of stories, their roots and musical characteristics are very similar. Both have had a big influence on today's pop music.

They are like two different sides of the same coin. Many important black musicians grew up singing the blues on Saturday night and gospel songs on Sunday morning, and the qualities of both kinds of music come together in their musical styles.

Plug In Again

Now write your own comparison-and-contrast essay. Compare two TV shows, books, movies, places to visit, applicants for a job, candidates for political office any two items that interest you. Decide whether your purpose is to evaluate, as Nadine's was; to inform, as Otis's was; or to persuade readers that they should agree with your preference or take a particular action. Try out your essay on a friend or colleague. Ask your reader to point out any places where he or she had trouble following your train of thought. Good luck!

CHAPTER TWENTY-THREE

The Cause-and-Effect Essay

Sometimes you have to write about why something has happened, or how particular causes have produced a particular effect. You might want to analyze why your company's year-end report was not done by the end of the year, explain how the colonists desire for freedom led to the American Revolution, or show how

underfunding of your children's school has led to lower-than-average test scores. Alternately, you might wish to write about what effect is likely to occur, given whatever causes you identify: "If we proceed with this new invoicing system, we can expect vendors to complain about the extra paperwork. We may even lose some of our smaller vendors, who don't have the staff to submit detailed invoices." Enter the cause-and-effect essay (or "c-and-e").

STEP ONE: THINK

Because questions about causes require solid logical reasoning, thinking plays a principal role in writing a cause-and-effect essay. Here are the do's and don'ts of effective c-and-e writing.

Don't confuse *sequence* with *cause*. "First I put on my lucky sweatsocks. Then I won three racquetball games in a row. Therefore, the sweatsocks *caused* me to win the games!" Probably not. If you wrote the above sentence (and we know that you didn't), your immediate task would be to isolate the *real* from the *apparent* causes of your stunning victory. Just because one event comes after another does not mean that the first event caused the second.

Give *specific evidence* to support your points. That means you may have to do some "homework" before writing. Read or research anything that will provide you with good supporting examples and evidence to use in your essay. For instance, say you are writing an essay explaining what you believe will happen if your company changes to a new invoicing system. You do a little research and find out what happened to another company in the same situation: "When the Coyote Company instituted a similar invoicing system, they lost three discount vendors in the first quarter. We are likely to encounter the same result." Now you sound like you know what you're talking about! If there's no time for research—as in a testing situation—make sure you choose a topic with which you are very familiar. Excuse the repetition, but if you do have time, do some reading on your subject. You'll be rewarded with a more convincing essay.

Distinguish among the different types of causes. A *remote cause* is related to an event, but far removed from it. An *underlying cause* is significant, but not immediately apparent to the casual observer. An *immediate* cause is the event that comes immediately before the effect. If you were writing about the Boston Tea Party, for example, the immediate cause would be the tax on tea, while an underlying cause would be the colonists' growing dissatisfaction with British rule. A remote cause might be the fact that some colonists from France and Germany disliked the British even before they arrived in America. Decide which causes are important enough to mention, and help your reader understand the relative weight of each.

There are three basic ways to organize a cause-and-effect essay.

1. *The cause-effect pattern*—First you state the causes, then you name the effect(s). Cynthia used a graphic organizer to identify this pattern as she prepared a memo describing her proposals for improving employee morale in her department:

Causes

- Abolish time clocks/put employees on honor system

- Increase lunch break from 45 minutes to one hour

- Offer an additional coffee break in the afternoon

Effect

- Improved employee morale

2. *The effect-cause pattern*—State the effect, then describe its causes. Here's Eric's chart, showing the causes for the Civil War:

CIVIL WAR

Causes

- arguments over slavery

- economic conflict between North and South

- Southern fears of losing political power

Effect

- war between the Union and the Confederacy

Note that if you use either of the first two patterns, you can list your causes in chronological order (first cause through last cause); reverse chronological order (last cause through first cause); or ascending order of importance (least important to most important).

 229

3. *The cause-effect chain*—Show how each effect becomes a cause leading to another effect. Marisol came up with this list of causes and effects to show how Lyme disease is spreading in her neighborhood:

Cause:	Starlings take over local cow barns.
Effect/Cause:	Farmers poison starlings.
Effect/Cause:	Dead starlings poison hawks.
Effect/Cause:	Hawks die off.
Effect/Cause:	Without hawks, mice population explodes.
Effect/Cause:	More mice to pass deer ticks to humans.
Final Effect:	Lyme disease increases.

STEP TWO: ACT

Write an introduction that will capture readers' attention or arouse their curiosity by letting them know *why* they should be interested in your topic. Marisol has an easy job. People in her community will want to know that her essay will help them avoid a nasty disease. And as with any essay, state your thesis clearly in your introductory paragraph.

In the body of your essay, it is essential to be consistent. Stick to the organization and order you chose. Also, be sure to include enough examples to illustrate each of your points. The major pitfall with a c-and-e essay is inadequate support for points made, so make those examples concrete and familiar.

In your conclusion, restate your thesis and let readers know how they can benefit from the information you gave them.

STEP THREE: REPAIR

If you have neglected to use transitions to show cause-and-effect relationships, add them now. Here, as elsewhere, they help readers follow your argument. The following transitional words and phrases are particularly useful in a c-and-e essay:

Useful Transitional Words to Show Cause and Effect

Cause

because, since, due to, for this (that) reason, this (that) is how, if . . . then

Effect

consequently, so, thus, as a result, therefore, nevertheless, for, so that

Check to make sure you have included enough examples to illustrate your points. You may have to add some now. (Do some additional "homework" if necessary.) You may also have to add definitions or explanations for any terms you may have used that might be unfamiliar to readers.

Finally, make sure you have not included any causes that are not real causes! Remember the lucky socks? And don't forget that "effect" is a noun meaning *something that happens as the result of a cause,* and "affect" is a verb meaning *to have an effect on.*

Cause-and-Effect Essay Checklist. When you edit and revise a c-and-e, follow these considerations:

- Does my introduction give an overview of my ideas in the form of a one- or two-sentence thesis statement?
- Have I identified which causes are *immediate,* which are *underlying,* and which are *remote ?*
- Have I chosen a clear and effective way of organizing my essay?
- Have I chosen the most effective order for the causes or effects I list?
- Have I used transition words to make clear the relationships between causes and effects?
- Have I provided enough details and examples to support my ideas?
- Have I included only *real* causes?
- Does my conclusion leave my readers with a clear understanding of my ideas?
- Does my conclusion let readers know how they will benefit from sharing my ideas?

Plug In

Marisol lives in eastern Pennsylvania, where Lyme disease was getting out of control. She and a group of concerned neighbors researched the problem. Then Marisol wrote the following rough draft of a position paper for her group, with the purpose of persuading readers that government officials needed to take action. Help Marisol edit her work, and then take a look at our comments.

Hints: Marisol needs help knowing where to start new paragraphs. She could also use some transition words. She might have left out some steps, or put them in the wrong order. Finally, she needs to keep her purpose in mind—not just to inform, but to persuade government officials to help.

Many people are not aware that the reason for the rising incidence of Lyme disease in our community is the use of a new pesticide. Local farmers, fed up with cleaning up after flocks of starlings that had invaded their bans, decided to kill the birds using this poison. They disposed of the dead birds on the manure piles in their back fields. The hawks absorbed the poison through their intestines and died in great numbers. The scarcity of hawks led to an explosion in the population of field mice. The incidence of Lyme disease in the area this spring has reached an all-time high. These field mice often carry deer ticks into villages and towns.

Plug In Solution

Now compare your edits to Marisol's final draft. What do you think of the end result?

Parents in our community have been alarmed by the rising incidence of Lyme disease in eastern Pennsylvania. Levels of this illness have reached frightening proportions. Solving this problem will require the cooperation of county officials with the state Department of Environmental Protection.

Many people are not aware that one reason for the disease's rising incidence is the use of a new pesticide. Local farmers, tired of cleaning up after the flocks of starlings that had invaded their barns, decided to kill the birds, using this poison. Unfortunately, they then disposed of the dead birds on the manure piles in their back fields.

As a result, the local hawks had easy access to the poisoned starlings. The hawks absorbed the poison through their intestines and consequently died in great numbers. The scarcity of hawks led to an explosion in the population of field mice, a common prey of hawks. These field mice often carry deer ticks infected with Lyme disease into the villages and towns.

Thus, the incidence of Lyme disease in the area this spring has reached an all-time high. As you can see, the solution is simple: Farmers must stop using the new pesticide. County and state officials must work with farmers to help them find other ways to deal with the starlings.

Plug In Again

Now write your own cause-and-effect essay. You can pick a topic of your choice or practice by explaining the causes for a time that you were late to school or work. Make sure readers can understand the order in which each cause happened, its relative importance, and the reason it produced its particular effect.

CHAPTER TWENTY-FOUR

The Problem-and-Solution Essay

We don't really have to define a problem-and-solution essay; the name says it all. You state a problem, you give the solution. The basic formula: state a problem and give an overview of the solution in your introduction; explain the solution and show why it will work in approximately three paragraphs; drive the point home in your conclusion.

Most of the time, problem-and-solution essays are written in response to actual, current problems. However, this form of essay might also serve if you're writing a paper for history or social studies. You might consider the problem faced by a particular historical figure and either analyze that person's solution or propose a solution of your own. If you were writing about Abraham Lincoln, for example, you might consider the problems he faced trying to keep the Union together before the Civil War. You might analyze the success or failure of his solutions while offering possible alternative solutions. Now, on to the mechanics of piecing this type of essay together . . . .

STEP ONE: THINK

If you're thinking graphically, you could start by making a pro-and-con chart, or a problem-and-solution chart, as in chapter 9.

If you're in list mode, try this: Nadine was trying to solve the problem of lateness in her company. Although the workday began at 9, too many employees were showing up at 9:15, 9:30, or even 9:45. She listed three possible solutions:

- Dock employees one fourth of an hour's wage for every 15 minutes they are late
- Give employees an extra hour's pay for every week in which they are on time every single day
- Have supervisors meet with any employee who is late two times in two weeks to discuss the problem

Then Nadine considered each solution from three points of view: that of employees, supervisors, and the company's top management.

Solution 1: Dock pay

1. Employees will be angry.

2. Supervisors might be happy if employees come on time; might be unhappy if employees are too angry and morale goes down.

3. Management will like the savings; may be concerned about lowered morale.

Solution 2: Reward punctuality

1. Employees will love this.

2. Supervisors will like happy, on-time employees.

3. Management won't want to spend money to reward people for doing what they're supposed to do anyway.

Solution 3: Supervisors meet with employees

1. Employees may respond well to personal approach

2. Supervisors may find burdensome; may like results

3. Management will be happy if this works—costs no money!

Because her analysis revealed that no one solution would satisfy everyone completely, Nadine decided not to make her own recommendation for a particular solution. Rather, she planned an essay that would analyze both problems and possible solutions, so that top management could make its own decision. Her purpose, then, was strictly to *inform*. If she had chosen a particular solution, her purpose might have been *to persuade* top management to adopt that approach.

A problem-and-solution, or p-and-s, essay, like a c-and-e essay, requires tight logical organization. A formal outline is strongly recommended.

Here are three possible organizations:

- If you have a *three-step solution* for a problem, use the basic formula. Identify the problem and give an overview of the solution in your introduction; then discuss each solution fully in a separate paragraph.

- If you, like Nadine, have *three possible solutions* to suggest, introduce the problem and the possible solutions in the introduction. Mention in your thesis statement that you are going to lay out the three possibilities, but leave it to your readers to decide which solution to adopt. In the body, write one paragraph for each possible solution, explaining the solution's pros and cons.

- If your solution has just *one step*, explain it in the introduction and, using ascending order of importance, write a paragraph for each major reason that your solution will work.

STEP TWO: ACT

Begin by *introducing the problem*. Let readers know why it is important. You may want to gather some facts and statistics to illustrate the gravity of the problem. Then, in a thesis statement, briefly preview the solution or solutions you are recommending.

Go on to *present your solution*, along with practical suggestions for how to implement it. Again, facts, statistics, examples, or quotations might help convince your readers. Even if they are already convinced, they might need supporting material so that they can convince others.

Imagine the objections that your readers might have to your solution. Briefly acknowledge these counter arguments and explain why your solution is still the best. If, like Nadine, you're describing several solutions, you should give the

pros and cons for each one and help your reader weigh these opposing arguments.

End with a strong conclusion that drives home your point. Once again, a fact, question, example, or quotation might speak to your readers more powerfully than a mere statement.

STEP THREE: REPAIR

Your first repair job is to read very carefully for any irrelevant information and ruthlessly cut it out. Next, make sure there are no holes in your arguments. If there are some, you'll have to fill them in with compelling reasons or facts.

∽〰○ **POWER LINE** ○〰∽

Not that the story need be long, but it will take a long while to make it short.

—Henry David Thoreau

If your writing sounds choppy and disconnected, it is possible that you have not used enough transitions. The ones that are most useful for problem-and-solution essays are: *because, thus, if . . . then, therefore, since, so, consequently, accordingly, as a result, for that reason, owing to.*

Choppiness can also be caused by short, disconnected sentences. If this is your problem, try combining some of those short sentences into one. Leave a few shorter sentences for variety. And speaking of variety, if your sentences all begin with the subject, revise some of them to liven up a monotonous style.

Use strong, direct words to convey to readers that the problem and its solution are important to them. A thesaurus will help you find stronger synonyms for weak words. For example, if you write, "Losing our wetlands would be *terrible*," you could use a thesaurus to find a synonym for the general, over-used word terrible. Then you might revise the sentence to read, "Losing our wetlands would be *disastrous*," or, "Losing our wetlands would be *tragic*."

Problem-and-Solution Essay Checklist. When you edit and revise a p-and-s, follow these considerations:

- Have I clearly identified the problem?
- Have I given an overview of the solution in my introduction?
- Is my introduction strong enough to convince readers that the problem is serious?
- Have I explained my solution clearly, with strong arguments, examples, and facts to back it up?
- Are my arguments logical and compelling?
- Have I anticipated and responded to possible objections to my solution?
- Have I concluded with a powerful statement, question, fact, quotation, or other device to drive home my point to my readers?
- Have I used strong, specific, direct language, avoiding words that are vague or overused?

Plug In

Here is the first draft of Nadine's memo about employee lateness, which she is planning to send to her company's top management. Help her edit it, then compare your work with ours. Hint: Take a quick look at Kaplan's Rules for Writing in Section I before you start editing!

TO: President Soto, Vice President Strauss, Secretary Chang

FROM: Nadine Rich, Personnel Manager

RE: Employee lateness

Our company is facing a serious problem. Employees seem to think they can wander into work just about any time they feel like it, no matter how late in the morning it is or what work might be waiting on their desks for them when they get there. It's becoming a real hassle for pretty much every department (except my own, of course).

I don't know why this is happening, and frankly, I don't care. I just want to make it stop. Here are three possible approaches we might choose to implement, depending on our analysis of their benefits and disadvantages at the present time.

1. We could dock their pay based on how late they are. For example, if someone is one quarter of an hour late, they lose one quarter of an hour's pay. If they're half an hour late, they lose half an hour's pay, and so on.

   Of course, the employees will just hate this, and it might be bad for morale. Our department heads won't be too happy if morale goes down. Sometimes, though, you just have to get tough. Why should we pay them for time they don't work?

2. We could give them an hour's pay for every week without lateness. Maybe we should go for the carrot instead of the stick. However, I can see that there might be objections to paying people for work they don't do. They're supposed to be on time anyway, aren't they? However, if this raises morale, and ends lateness, it might be worth it.

3. Supervisors might meet with any employees who is late more than two times in two weeks. This would signal a get tough approach without actually punishing anyone. Employees might respond well to this approach, and of course, it won't cost any money. However, our department heads may not like the extra work, and some people just don't like to discipline others. Still, if that's how they feel, maybe they shouldn't be department heads.

Well, that's my thinking. What's yours?

Plug In Solution

Here's Nadine's final draft. What do you think? Do you see why certain changes were made?

TO: President Soto, Vice President Strauss, Secretary Chang

FROM: Nadine Rich, Personnel Manager

RE: Employee lateness

Our company is facing a serious problem. Employees in virtually every department are regularly coming in from 15 to 45 minutes late. A brief survey of department heads shows that at least 75 percent of the employees in each department are at least 15 minutes late at least twice a week, while almost 40 percent are at least half an hour late at least once a week. I estimate that this is costing us some 30 hours of lost time per week—almost a full work week!

Department heads were not able to explain the reasons for this problem. This in itself is significant: Clearly, department heads are not talking to their employees about the lateness. Clearly, too, employees are not receiving the message from their supervisors that this lateness is unacceptable.

Under the circumstances, I can think of three possible approaches we might take:

1. We could dock employees' pay based on how late they are. Once an employee is more than 15 minutes late, he or she might lose a quarter of an hour's pay. Each additional 15 minutes lateness would cost another quarter-hour's pay.

   Of course, employees will resent this, and it might be bad for morale. Supervisors might therefore be unhappy with this solution. However, this is a serious problem, so perhaps we need show employees and supervisors that we are serious about it.

2. We could give employees an hour's pay for every week without lateness. You may object to paying people for work they don't do. However, if this measure raises morale while ending lateness, it might be worth the cost.

3. Supervisors might meet with any employee who is late more than twice in two weeks. Our department heads may not feel comfortable with this approach, particularly since it requires them to discipline employees.

However, department heads are responsible for supervising their workers. This policy would signal how serious we are without actually punishing anyone. Employees might respond well to this approach, and of course, it won't cost any money.

Whatever we decide, we need to move fast. Every week that goes by represents 30 hours of employee time lost through lateness.

Plug In Again

Write your own problem-and-solution essay. You might choose a problem you take seriously—a difficulty at work, an environmental concern, or the problem facing an historical figure. Or, just for fun, choose a humorous problem: the alarming outbreak of plastic containers in your refrigerator, each filled with a mysterious substance, for example. Show why this problem is deadly serious, what solution might address it, and how the solution could be carried out.

CHAPTER TWENTY-FIVE

Other Essays

There are three other types of essays that we'll touch on briefly here:

- Personal response to literature
- Interpretation of literature
- Comparative analysis of two or more works of literature

Note that most of what we say in this chapter applies to film, television, music, and other types of art, as well as to literature. For convenience, we've just called it literature (although one of the sample essays is about television). The same basic principles apply, though, so rely on these pointers for your art history, music appreciation, and pop culture courses, as well as for English and Lit.

WRITING WELL FOR TESTS AND ASSIGNMENTS

The process of writing a paper and the procedure for answering an essay test question are similar. In both cases, you should rely upon the writing process: Think, Act, Repair. In both cases, you should identify a thesis statement and make sure that every sentence in every paragraph relates to that thesis.

Tips for Writing Test Essays. Here are a few extra pointers for essay questions on tests:

- Make sure you understand exactly what the question means. It helps to restate the question in your own words, either in your own mind or on scratch paper.

- If possible, have some scratch paper handy to jot down your thesis statement and make a brief outline. If this is not allowed, make some very light notes in pencil in a corner of your test paper and erase them later.

- Time yourself. Figure out how long you should spend on each question. Then divide up the time you've allotted to each question. For a 20-minute question, for example, plan to spend about five minutes on prewriting, 13 minutes on drafting, and two minutes on revising and editing.

- When you think about your audience and purpose, don't kid yourself. If you are writing for a school assignment or test, your principal audience is your teacher, and one of your purposes is to show your teacher (a) that you can express your ideas in writing, and (b) that you understood the work of literature well enough to have ideas in the first place. These are perfectly legitimate purposes, and you should keep them in mind as your write.

Avoid a Pesky Mistake

There's one really pesky mistake that many writers make when writing about literature. They are never sure whether to use present or past tense when writing about events in a book or film. You can see where the confusion comes from. If you are writing about events in a book that has (obviously) already been written, especially if the book was written a hundred years ago, it seems funny to put your writing about them in the present tense. For example, "In Jane Austen's novel *Sense and Sensibility*, Elizabeth makes/made a mistake in her judgment of Mr. Darcy"; or "Jane Austen makes/made women her most interesting characters."

Here is the solution: Just be consistent. It does not matter whether you use the past or the present (actually, the *present* is preferred), just so you do not keep switching back and forth. Before you start, make up your mind if you are going to write about literary characters and events in the present or past. Then stick to your decision.

YOUR PERSONAL RESPONSE TO LITERATURE

Sometimes you may be asked to write your own personal response to a work of literature. Your assignment might be as general as, "Share your personal response to Jane Austen's *Sense and Sensibility*," or as specific as, "Explain which of Jane Austen's novels has more relevance to your own life: *Pride and Prejudice* or *Sense and Sensibility*." Your assignment could also take the form, "Explain why you did or did not enjoy reading Jane Austen's *Emma*." In either case, your purpose is to express your thoughts and feelings about what you have read to a larger community of writers and readers that includes your teacher and possibly your classmates.

 **POWER LINE**

'Tis the good reader who makes the good book.

—Ralph Waldo Emerson

The key to writing a good response is to *be specific*. Tell exactly how the work made you feel and precisely what thoughts it stirred in you. Use language that is specific and concrete rather than general, vague, or abstract.

> **General Response:** I liked this book because even though it was sad, it had a happy ending.

> **Specific Response:** I liked this book because it made me feel both sad and hopeful about love. The writer captured my own feelings of loss and emptiness after losing someone I cared about. Yet the story's ending proved that love is worthwhile, even when the loved one is gone.

If you are responding to the work by evaluating it, as in the example above, go on to provide *concrete examples from the work itself* to back up your points. You might, in addition, include quotations from other works or from other critics. While it is acceptable to cite a personal experience related to the literature, be careful to keep your focus on the literature, not on thoughts about your own life. Now let's go through the writing process for a personal response to a work of literature (which you can apply to any essay for tests or school assignments).

Step One: Think

Answering one or more of these open-ended questions can help you find a topic for a response to literature:

 245

- What in this work surprised me?
- What characters, events, or scenes reminded me of events in my own life? How did they make me feel about my own life? Did they shed new light on any of my own experiences?
- What characters, events, or scenes were completely new to me? What new thoughts or feelings did they inspire?
- What other books (or other works of art) was I reminded of?
- What images are still with me?
- What about the work upset me?
- Do I agree or disagree with the writer's view of the world? Why?

Some writers find it useful to focus these open-ended questions with follow-up questions. Here is how Ralph used this process as he prepared to write a personal response to Jane Austen's novel *Sense and Sensibility:*

Open-Ended Question: What images are still with me?

Strong Reaction: When Elinor is so excited after Edward finally proposes to her and she realizes that he didn't marry Lucy after all.

Follow-up Question: Why does Elinor's excitement make such an impression on me?

Focused Response: It shows that sometimes, true love is rewarded. I like that idea, and that's why I liked this book so much.

Eventually, you need to focus your response to literature in the form of a thesis statement—a one- or two-sentence statement of your main idea. Here are some thesis statements that Ralph considered. Notice that the first focuses on character, the second on plot or theme, the third on historical background. Ralph might also have chosen to write about Jane Austen's language, her descriptions of England, or any other aspect of the novel that moved him.

Sense and Sensibility is a fascinating character study. I started out liking Marianne best, but ended up having more respect for Elinor.

I liked *Sense and Sensibility* because it shows that love can succeed if a person loves for the right reasons.

246

Sense and Sensibility upset me because it was painful to read about women whose main goal in life was to get married before the age of 20.

Step Two: Act

Once you have chosen your topic and written your thesis statement, your next task is to help readers understand your response to the work.

Start by summarizing or giving readers background information they will need if they haven't read the book you are discussing. Be brief, but include enough information to help readers follow any points you make later. For example, if Ralph's focus is his reaction to the historical background, he should describe the novel's setting: "Marianne and Elinor live in a world in which a woman is considered an old maid if she isn't married by age 20."

Cite examples and quote from the book wherever possible. If you think a book is funny, describe a comic scene or a quote a humorous bit of dialogue. If you like the author's viewpoint, explain some of his or her ideas. You might also *paraphrase,* or retell, episodes in words that convey your own point of view. If Ralph admires Elinor, for example, he might write: "In a moving passage, the wise Elinor pleads with her foolish sister to be more careful." If Ralph dislikes the character of Elinor, he might describe the same scene very differently: "In a particularly irritating passage, the timid, smug Elinor tries to talk her passionate sister out of following her heart." Be sure to tell *why* the work affected you: Because it reminded you of someone you know? Because it made you think about death? Because you felt sorry for the characters? Because it gave you hope for true love?

Step Three: Repair

When you read over your response, pretend that you have never read the book, or find a reader who really hasn't read the book and ask for his or her reaction to your writing. Your reader should get a general idea of what the book is about and be able to follow your arguments or examples. If your reader has trouble following your writing, find out where the trouble spots are and revise.

When reading your work for grammar, spelling, and punctuation errors (Stage Three revision), pay particular attention to punctuating quotations correctly. If you are unsure of the rules, look them up in a grammar book or a style manual.

"Personal Response to Literature" Essay Checklist. When you edit and revise a personal response to literature, whether for a test or a school assignment, follow these considerations:

- Does my thesis statement make my response to this work clear?
- Have I included background information about the book so that readers who have not read it will be able to follow my thoughts?
- Have I been careful to keep my writing focused on the book rather than on my own personal experiences?
- Are my explanations clear and concise?
- Have I included examples and quotations from the book to back up my point of view?
- Have I checked grammar, spelling, and punctuation, especially the use of punctuation in quotations?

Plug In

Here is Ralph's first draft of his personal response to *Sense and Sensibility.* Help him edit it, then take a look at our final draft. Keep these three principles in mind:

- The purpose of the essay is to share the writer's personal response to a work of literature.
- The thesis statement gives an overview of the writer's response.
- Every sentence should support the thesis statement.
- Examples, quotations, and paraphrases can help bring ideas to life.

Sense and Sensibility: A Practical Romance

Is it possible to be in love and still to keep both feet planted firmly on the ground? Jane Austen says it is.

The novel is the story of two sisters, Elinor and Marianne. To be honest, I had a lot more sympathy with Marianne when the book started. No way will she marry boring old Colonel Brandon, who is much older than she is. She falls in love with Willoughby. Elinor loves Edward, but suffers in silence when it looks like he's engaged to another woman.

Like I said, I have always agreed with Marianne—I have always thought passion was the most important ingredient of love. So at first I didn't like the way Austen kept praising Elinor. Just because she was so sensible! But when I saw the terrible things that happened to Marianne, and the way that Elinor was rewarded, I started to wonder whether I was too much like Marianne. By the time the novel was over, Austen had convinced me that Elinor's way was better. I really did not expect this.

I also really liked the descriptions of the English countryside. It made me feel like I had visited a whole other country—a really beautiful country.

I guess I still hope that love can have both passion and good sense. But then, Elinor has passion. That's what changed my mind—seeing how deeply she cared about Edward and how happy she was when they finally got together.

Besides, Marianne does end up feeling passionate about the old Colonel. That's why I liked *Sense and Sensibility* so much—it taught me that you can be a down-to-earth, practical person and still find true love.

Plug In Solution

It's Ralph's final draft. What do you think of it?

Sense and Sensibility: A Practical Romance

Is it possible to be in love and still to keep both feet planted firmly on the ground? Jane Austen says it is in her classic novel Sense and Sensibility. This book taught me that you can be a down-to-earth, practical person and still find true love.

The novel is the story of two sisters, the sensible, practical Elinor, and impulsive, passionate Marianne. When the novel began, I had far more sympathy with Marianne. She refuses to marry the boring Colonel Brandon, who is much older than she is, and falls in love with the romantic Willoughby. Elinor, meanwhile, loves Edward, but suffers in silence when he seems to be engaged to another woman. Eventually, though, Willoughby turns out to be a cad, Elinor and Edward are happily reunited, and Marianne sees the error of her ways and marries Colonel Brandon.

I have always agreed with Marianne—I have always thought passion was the most important ingredient of love. So when Austen kept praising Elinor's ability to "govern" her feelings, I kept wanting to argue with her.

Then I saw how much Marianne suffered when Willoughby turned out to be a cad. I realized that if she had been more careful, she might not have been so badly hurt. I began to wonder whether I was too much like Marianne.

I saw, too, that Elinor did feel passion. When Edward finally proposes to her, she nearly faints from joy. By the time the novel was over, I was surprised to find that Austen had convinced me: Elinor's way was better.

The final proof is that even Marianne combines love and good sense. She marries the worthy Colonel Brandon, but, Austen tells us, "Marianne could never love by halves; and her whole being became, in time, as much devoted to her husband as it had been to Willoughby." That's why I liked Sense and Sensibility so much: It gave me hope that love can include both passion and respect.

YOUR INTERPRETATION OF LITERATURE

An *interpretation* explores the meaning of a work. The writer helps readers to better understand the work or appreciate it in a new way. In an interpretive essay, the writer closely examines a work of literature to explore its meaning and develop an opinion about what the writer was really saying. Then he or she goes on to back up that opinion with evidence.

While there may be no right or wrong interpretation for a work of literature, an interpretation may be *valid* or *invalid*. For example, say you and your friend go to a movie, an adventure story in which two guys compete for the love of a woman while trying to battle an evil intergalactic empire. (Okay, you

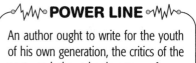 **POWER LINE**

An author ought to write for the youth of his own generation, the critics of the next, and the schoolmasters of ever afterward.

–F. Scott Fitzgerald

caught us. It's *Star Wars*.) You think Luke Skywalker is the real hero of the movie, and you hope he ends up with Princess Leia. Your friend thinks Han Solo is the hero and argues that *he* deserves the princess's love. While the two of you are arguing, you run into your cousin Arnold. *He* argues that the movie's true hero is R2D2, the lovable robot. Now we have three opinions about the movie. You and your friend have *valid* opinions; that is, whether or not we agree with either of them, there is plenty of evidence to support them. Arnold's opinion is *invalid* (sorry, Arnold) because he could not back it up with concrete evidence.

In further discussion, you argue that the movie is really about Luke's quest for his own identity, while your friend says it is about Han's need to learn humility. Both of you have evidence from the movie to support your points of view. But when you ask Arnold why he thinks the movie is about R2D2, he says, "I don't know, I just like him." You lose again, Arnold. That is not interpretation. When you interpret a movie, book, or any work of art, you do more than just state your opinion. You make a good case for that opinion, using concrete examples.

There are three ways to support your interpretation:

- With *evidence* from the work itself: "As soon as Han admits he has made a mistake, the Princess likes him better."

 251

- With *examples from related works:* "Many hero tales require the hero to learn humility before winning true love."
- With *examples from personal experience:* "No self-respecting woman like Princess Leia would let a man get away with acting the way Han does."

Step One: Think

To find a topic for your interpretive essay, take notes as you read. Jot down the questions and reactions that occur to you. As you read over your notes, think about which aspect or element of the work you would like to write about.

Here is a list of aspects of literary works along with the questions you might ask about them. Feel free to write about other elements, to create your own questions, and to adapt these questions to other works of art, such as movies, plays, television shows, music, paintings, and sculpture.

Elements

Plot	Tone	Thesis/Theme
Characters	Symbols	
Setting/Atmosphere	Title	

Questions

- What is the work's main conflict? What causes the conflict? What larger issue is conveyed through the conflict?
- Why does a particular character behave in a certain way? What does the character learn? What message is the author conveying through that character?
- Why did the author choose this particular setting/atmosphere? What does it contribute to the work?
- What is the author's tone? How does the tone affect the work?
- What does a particular symbol mean? What does it tell us about the message that the author wants to convey?

- How does the title reveal the larger meaning of the work? How does the title help us understand the work's events?
- What is the author's central insight?

Next, create a thesis statement. Celia, who decided to write about the author's central insight in *Sense and Sensibility*, wrote this: "Jane Austen believes in *sense*, which she defines as moderation and prudence, and distrusts *sensibility*, which she defines as a passionate, emotional response to life."

To organize her ideas, Celia made a large Venn diagram (see chapter 9, Organizing Your Ideas). Beneath one circle she wrote "Elinor," and beneath the other, "Marianne." She listed the character traits the two sisters had in common in the center of the diagram, and the qualities she could ascribe to one or the other in the appropriate circles.

Then she went back to the book to find and list examples that would support her claims for each character. When she writes, she will choose three major ways (three paragraphs) in which to compare and contrast the two sisters, proving that Jane Austen chose the sister with "sense" to be the more successful in life.

Step Two: Act

In your introductory paragraph, include the name of the work, the author, any essential background information, and your thesis statement. If necessary, summarize the work or provide any other information about it that readers will need to follow your argument. For example, if you are focusing on a character, describe the character. If your emphasis is on a plot event, tell that part of the story.

Most of the body of your essay will include arguments, quotations, paraphrases (restating something in your own words), and other evidence from the work to support your thesis. You can also bring in comparisons and contrasts to other works ("Unlike Charlotte Brontë, whose most sympathetic characters are deeply passionate, Jane Austen essentially mistrusted intense feeling, placing her faith in cool reason."). It is also acceptable to use personal experience or general observations to support your arguments—but be careful. If your tone is too personal, your readers may take you less seriously or find it easier to disagree with you.

In your conclusion, summarize your interpretation, perhaps referring to the strongest evidence for your case. As always, avoid starting any new arguments or bringing in evidence that we have not heard before.

Step Three: Repair

We think it is helpful to show an interpretive essay to someone else who has read (or seen) the work you are discussing. Ask your reader to restate your point of view in his or her own words. Then ask your reader where your arguments were convincing and where they seemed vague, illogical, or unsupported by evidence.

You don't have to take your reader's word as gospel; all readers have their own interpretations, after all. But your reader might help you pinpoint some places where you could make a stronger case for your ideas.

"Interpretation of Literature" Essay Checklist. When you edit and revise an interpretation of literature, follow these considerations:

- Is my interpretation reasonable and valid? Can it be backed up with concrete evidence?
- Have I limited my interpretation to one aspect of the work?
- Does my thesis statement clearly state the main idea of my essay?
- Does my introduction include the name and author of the work?
- Does my introduction include sufficient background information for readers who have not read the work?
- Have I supplied ample evidence to support my interpretation?
- Are my arguments logical and convincing?
- Have I written a strong conclusion that will invite readers to think more about my ideas?

Plug In

Here's Celia's interpretive essay on *Sense and Sensibility*. We included it because we wanted you to contrast it to Ralph's personal response to the same novel. Edit Celia's rough draft, check out our final draft, and then look at Ralph's personal response from earlier in the chapter to see the difference between a personal response and an interpretive essay.

The Conflict Between "Sense" and "Sensibility"

Jane Austen believes in sense and distrusts sensibility. In *Sense and Sensibility*, Elinor represents sense, while Marianne represents sensibility.

It would be too simple to say that Elinor is rewarded while Marianne is punished. After all, Elinor suffers for most of the novel. But Marianne suffers too. And of course, Elinor has a happy ending. But so does Marianne.

The point is that Marianne gets a happy ending only when she realizes the error of her ways and starts acting like Elinor. Then she is happy. This is Austen's way of telling us that even in the face of unhappy love, sense is the way to go. Sense will get you through bad times a lot better than sensibility will. When Elinor looks back at her conduct, she can be proud of how she acted. But Marianne is ashamed. That's because she lacked sense.

In my opinion, then, Austen wants to say that sense is better than sensibility. As she puts it, "Marianne Dashwood was born to an extraordinary fate. She was born to discover the falsehood of her own opinions . . . "

255

Plug In Solution

Here's Celia's final draft. Your opinion?

The Conflict Between "Sense" and "Sensibility"

Jane Austen believes in sense—moderation and prudence—and distrusts sensibility—a passionate, emotional response to life. Nowhere is this conflict more clear than in her novel, *Sense and Sensibility.* In this story of two young sisters in love, Elinor represents sense, while Marianne represents sensibility. (In Austen's time, the word sensibility meant "the ability to feel deeply and passionately, often with the senses.")

It would be too simple to say that Elinor is rewarded while Marianne is punished. True, Marianne falls in love with a man who turns out to be a cad. But Elinor also suffers for most of the novel: She is in love with a man whom she believes is promised to another. And despite their different approaches to life, both women are rewarded at the end of the novel with happy marriages.

But Elinor gets her reward because of her sense. Marianne is rewarded despite her sensibility. In fact, Marianne gets her happy ending only when she realizes the error of her ways and starts acting like Elinor. She finds true happiness when she marries an upright, reliable man—someone Elinor approves of, someone she herself once scorned. As Austen puts it, "Marianne Dashwood was born to an extraordinary fate. She was born to discover the falsehood of her own opinions . . . "

Moreover, when Elinor looks back at her conduct, she can be proud of how she acted. But Marianne is ashamed of her impulsive, emotional behavior: "I saw that my own feelings had prepared by sufferings and that my want of fortitude under them had almost led me to the grave." This is Austen's way of telling us that even in the face of unhappy love, sense is more reliable than sensibility.

Thus, while both women suffer and both women end happily, Austen still makes her point. Sense is rewarded, while sensibility only brings needless suffering.

YOUR COMPARATIVE ANALYSIS

A *comparative analysis* is a type of essay that compares two or more items in a way that brings out surprising or meaningful aspects of both. The point of this type of essay is to make a point or draw a conclusion about the literature based on the results you find. One thing we should mention is that, although we have defined *comparison* as finding *similarities,* and *contrast* as finding *differences,* here we throw caution to the winds and just use the term "comparative analysis" to mean *an essay that analyzes both similarities and differences.*

Step One: Think

An ideal topic for a comparative analysis is two items that are related to each other, but in not too obvious a way. No one, for example, will be surprised to find that two plays by Shakespeare are similar or that a Shakespeare play is very different from an episode of *Friends.* But

⌐∿∿° **POWER LINE** °∿∿⌐

There is only one trait that marks the writer. He is always watching. It's a kind of trait of mind and he is born with it.

—Morley Callaghan

pointing out significant differences between a character in an early Shakespeare play and a similar character in a later play might show one way in which Shakespeare had developed as a playwright over the years. Pointing out similarities between *Journal of the Plague Year* by Daniel Defoe (1660–1731) and a modern novel about AIDS might reveal some important insight into how human beings deal with plagues. On the other hand, discovering differences between the two works might bring out interesting insights into each historical period.

Here are some other examples of topics for comparative analyses:

- Compare the events in an author's life with certain incidents in his or her works.

- Contrast two works about the same historical figure, such as George Bernard Shaw's *St. Joan* and Jean Anouilh's *The Lark,* both plays about Joan of Arc.

- Compare one aspect of two different media, such as the narrative techniques used in fiction writing and filmmaking.

 **KAPLAN** 257

To help you develop ideas, you might use an idea cluster or word web. Write the name of each item you are comparing in the center of a separate sheet of paper and write ideas about each one in circles around it. Look for ideas on the two sheets that "match up," that is, lend themselves to comparison or contrast.

A formal outline to organize your ideas is recommended for a comparative analysis. Here is how you might set one up:

I. The items you will compare; a general overview of their similarities and differences
II. How your two items are different
   A. First difference
     1. example
     2. example
   B. Second difference
     1. example
     2. example
     3. example
III. One important way in which your two items are similar
   A. example
   B. example
   C. example
IV. Why the similarity between the two items is meaningful

Step Two: Act

Your introduction should clearly reveal to readers exactly which two items you will compare and contrast, and in which ways. For example: "Both *The Lark* and *St. Joan* are plays about Joan of Arc. Although Jean Anouilh treats his subject seriously, while George Bernard Shaw treats the same subject with a sense of humor, both see Joan of Arc as a tragic figure." Or: "While both fiction writing and filmmaking are narrative arts, that is, arts that tell stories, the craft of the fiction writer differs from that of the filmmaker in three important ways." In this type of essay, it is often best to save your thesis statement for the *end*. After you've compared and/or contrasted the two items may be the best time to reveal the significance of their similarities and/or differences.

In the body of your essay, cite examples in the form of quotations, plot developments, images, or descriptions that demonstrate how your items are similar and/or different. Organize your paragraphs so that you are "building a case" for your thesis statement, which will explain why the similarities and/or differences you have pointed out are significant. For example, the writer of the Joan of Arc essay might say something about the definition of tragedy; the writer of the fiction vs. film essay could use his or her evidence to claim that fiction writing is a more demanding craft than filmmaking—or vice versa.

Step Three: Repair

Read over your essay, pretending to be totally unfamiliar with the work or works the essay discusses. Do you feel that enough background information has been provided, or do you feel like asking the writer, "What are you talking about?" Avoid a "What are you talking about?" response by adding explanation and information where necessary.

In a comparative analysis, it's particularly important to make clear the relationships between your ideas. Transition words—*like, too, similarly, also, in the same way, just as, both, likewise*—show similarities. And use words that indicate differences, such as: *in contrast, however, but, on the other hand, conversely, whereas.*

Because you are writing about two items in the same essay, you have to be especially careful about clear pronoun reference. For example, read the following sentence: "Screen writing is more difficult than fiction writing because *it* requires more visual imagination on the part of the writer." To which kind of writing does the pronoun *it* refer? The rules of grammar say it refers to the closest noun—that would be fiction writing. But it sounds as if the writer meant it to refer to screen writing. Or maybe not. In any case, the writer should not have used a pronoun at all: "Screen writing is more difficult than fiction writing because writing for the screen requires more visual imagination on the part of the writer." Use pronouns only when their reference is perfectly clear.

Use the following checklist to be sure you've gone through all the stages of the repair process for a comparative analysis.

"Comparative Analysis" Checklist. When you edit and revise a comparative analysis, use our handy guidelines:

- Does my introduction clearly explain the two items I am comparing and contrasting?
- Does my organization let the reader follow my ideas easily?
- Have I given sufficient examples and other evidence to build my case for the upcoming thesis statement?
- Does my conclusion reveal why the similarities and/or differences between my two items are significant?
- Have I included sufficient background information to support readers who are not familiar with my subject matter?
- Have I used transitions to show the relationships between ideas?
- Have I eliminated all unclear pronoun references?

Plug In

For her "Media and Communications" course, Jeannie wrote this comparative analysis of two television programs. She needs help keeping her organization clear and consistent, so keep that in mind as you edit her rough draft. You might also point out places that you think she needs to add some examples or evidence. And keep an eye on her conclusion: Does she show why the connections she has discovered are significant? Then see how we edited her work, in the polished final draft.

From *The Honeymooners* to *Roseanne*: Television Grows Up

Imagine the pitch meeting: "Boss, I've got a great idea. We'll take that Jackie Gleason character from *The Honeymooners*—you know, loud, overweight, working class, funny—only this time, we'll make him a woman!" However, the differences between the two shows, however, reveal an enormous change in American television.

First, let's look at the similarities. Both *Roseanne* and *The Honeymooners* feature hardworking working-class families who are struggling just to survive and stay alive. The main character is in danger of losing their job. The main character is in a strong marriage with a supportive, loving, and sensible partner. But on *Roseanne*, the married couple is in danger.

Roseanne's main character is a woman. *The Honeymooners'* main character is a man. Although the Jackie Gleason character on *The Honeymooners* seemed to face economic disaster, everything always turned out all right in the end. On *Roseanne*, the characters really suffer. They show far more serious consequences of economic problems than anything on *The Honeymooners*.

Moreover, while the married couples on both shows fought, the "Honeymooners" always made up by the end of the half-hour.

For its time, *The Honeymooners* dealt with serious issues. But *Roseanne* is far more serious.

Plug In Solution

And here is Jeannie's final draft, her polished comparative analysis.

From *The Honeymooners* to *Roseanne*: Television Grows Up

Imagine the pitch meeting: "Boss, I've got a great idea. We'll take that Jackie Gleason character from *The Honeymooners*—you know, loud, overweight, working class, funny—only this time, we'll make him a woman!" When *Roseanne* first aired on network television, many people were comparing this situation comedy to *The Honeymooners*, even though the programs were some three decades apart. And indeed, there were many similarities between the two half-hour situation comedies. The differences between the two shows, however, reveal an enormous change in American television.

First, let's look at the similarities. Both *Roseanne* and *The Honeymooners* feature working-class families who are struggling just to survive. On both shows, the main character is in frequent danger of losing his or her job. And on both shows, the main character is in a strong marriage with a supportive, loving, and sensible partner.

However, *Roseanne's* main character is a woman, while *The Honeymooners'* main character is a man. Although the Jackie Gleason character on *The Honeymooners* seemed to face economic disaster—loss of employment, rent increases, high income-tax bills—everything always turned out all right in the end. On *Roseanne*, by contrast, the characters really suffer. In one episode, for example, we see how a failed business venture means that the couple's oldest daughter cannot go to college. This is a far more serious consequence of economic problems than anything ever shown on *The Honeymooners*.

Moreover, while the married couples on both shows fought, the "Honeymooners" always made up by the end of the half hour. On *Roseanne*, by contrast, even a loving married couple is shown to be in danger of separation and divorce.

For its time, *The Honeymooners* dealt with serious issues. But the far greater seriousness of *Roseanne* shows just how far television has come. The differences between these two apparently similar programs reveal a startling conclusion: Perhaps television has grown up.

REFERENCE
SECTION B

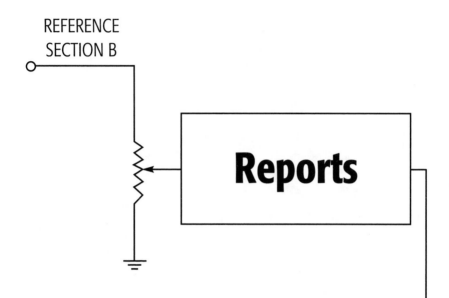

Reports

Writing a Report

Whether you are a student working on a research or lab report, or an employee whose boss has asked for a review or progress report, we think you'll find this section useful. In addition, if your on-the-job writing involves assimilating large amounts of information and presenting them in a report format, then this section will be very useful.

Warming Up. There are two kinds of reports described in this section: the research report and lab report. Look over the part that applies to your report.

Stretching. Skim the section you have chosen. Take a few notes or reread parts that are of special importance to the kind of report you are doing.

Working Out. Go back into other sections of this book to review what we mean by Think, Act, and Repair. Look for any other ideas in these sections that may apply to your report writing.

Training. Begin by doing the prewriting tasks. Make diagrams, charts, and outlines, and continue to brainstorm and narrow your topic lists.

Sprint. In a research report, you will spend a lot of time in the library or online doing your homework. In the lab report, you will conduct experiments.

Marathon. Write the report in rough draft. Use your outline and organization and go through it quickly but carefully.

Cooling Down. Let the report sit for a few days. Go back to it and rewrite it into a revised draft. Add or subtract, being careful to use precise and formal language.

Personal Best. Write the second draft, polish it up, run it off, and turn it in. You are done with this assignment and can relax.

REPORTS: THE INSIDE STORY

"Do a report on . . . ." Those words do not usually bring joy to your heart or put a spring in your step, do they? You envision long, tedious hours in the library or online, and then even longer, more tedious hours at your desk with a tangle of scrawled notes that you don't know what to do with. (Why is that when you take notes in the library, your handwriting begins to look more and more like a secret code from another planet?)

We hope you perk up a little when we tell you that, just as there's a formula for writing an essay, there's a formula for writing a report. Once you know the formula, you can follow it quite easily. We won't try to hide the fact that you still have to do your research, and that will take time, but we'll help you through that, too. And if you take your notes in our special, "proven effective" way, you'll end up with a report that's almost written! Honest.

THE THESIS STATEMENT, REVISITED

Remember our old friend, the thesis statement? Well, get ready to renew your friendship, because your report, like an essay, will be organized around a central thesis: an idea you intend to demonstrate or prove. To review briefly, a thesis statement is one or a few sentences at the beginning of your report that clearly and concisely state your main idea. In a research report, you'll use the findings of others to back up your thesis. In a lab report, you'll rely on your own findings. But in both cases, your writing task revolves around a central idea, or thesis, and evidence that supports it.

No matter how well written your thesis statement may be, it may not be a real attention-getter by itself. Here are some ways to highlight your thesis statement and turn it into a "must read" interest grabber:

- Maybe your main idea is fascinating in itself. If so, state it clearly and concisely right at the beginning of your report.

- Lead into your thesis statement with a question. Make it a question that will really get your readers thinking and make them curious about the answer. Hint that they will find the answer by reading your report.
- Include a fact or statistic that will surprise them and whet their appetites for more information.
- Introduce your thesis statement with a quotation by someone with whom your readers are familiar. Choose a quote that is catchy, clever, or surprising.
- Start off with an anecdote from your own experience or one that you have read. Make it short and pithy, and make sure it leads readers right into your thesis statement.

Let there be no doubt about the importance of a thesis statement in a report! For example, suppose you do extensive research into land holdings in seventeenth century Salem. You write up your research in a clear, accessible way. So, who cares? It's only when you say, "This report will demonstrate that the Salem witch trials were a result of legal battles over land ownership," that readers begin to see why your information is interesting. Or suppose you write up a detailed report on your experiments with teaching mice to go through a maze. "So what?" ask your readers. But if you first let them know that you're demonstrating a theory of learning that may be of use for humans, they know where you're going, and they're happy to follow you through all the information that you have to report.

THE PARAGRAPH, REVISITED

The paragraph is the basic unit of almost any piece of writing. For a reader, a skipped line or an indented sentence is an announcement that says, "Warning! New idea coming up!" So make sure that each of your paragraphs focuses on one main idea. In fact, think of a paragraph as a mini-essay or mini-report. Just like a whole piece of writing, it has an introduction, a body, and a conclusion; and it has a sentence (the topic sentence) that tells the main idea, just as an essay or report has a thesis statement. The big difference is that the conclusion of a paragraph needs to flow into the introduction of the next. That's where transitional words and phrases come in. If the term *transition* only rings a faint bell from the distant past, go back and review transitional words and phrases in the earlier chapters.

To Write a Great Report. We will make this short and sweet. Well-written paragraphs are the building blocks of a great report. As in an essay, each paragraph in your report should relate to or support your thesis statement. Moreover, each paragraph should center on one clear main idea, expressed in a topic sentence. The other sentences in the paragraph support that idea.

UNITY, COMPLETENESS, AND COHERENCE

One more quick review. Those three good things—unity, completeness, and coherence—are as essential for a good report as they are for a good essay. So let's go over them just once for good measure.

- To achieve *unity,* be sure there is nothing irrelevant in your report.
- To achieve *completeness,* make sure that no important information is missing.
- To achieve *coherence,* be sure that your paragraphs and sentences are written in a logical, easy-to-follow order.

And by the way, don't forget your secret weapon, the writing process: Think, Act, Repair. It works every time.

CHAPTER TWENTY-SIX

◦Research Reports

WHAT IS A RESEARCH REPORT?

A research report is basically a long essay, complete with introduction, body, and conclusion. Sound familiar so far? So why can't we just say, "To write a report, write an essay

◦◦◦ **POWER LINE** ◦◦◦

Writing is making sense of life.

—Nadine Gordimer

but make it longer"? Because there is one important difference. *In the body of your research report, you will not be supporting your thesis with ideas of your own, but with information gathered from a variety of sources,* usually including books and magazine articles, and sometimes including newspaper articles, interviews, or speeches. In addition, you need to include in your report *documentation* on where you got your information, so that interested readers could check your sources out for themselves. (Don't get nervous. We'll go through all this step by step.)

Before even talking about the definition of a research report, we have one very important piece of advice. *Don't* start at the last minute! As you read on, you'll see that to write a good report, you'll need as much time as you can get.

- You will need time to do research at the library, or perhaps even at more than one library. You will also need time to go back if you find you are missing an important piece of information.
- You will need time to take careful notes and time to organize them carefully.

If you have time for all this, we guarantee your report will be much better organized and better written than if you have to rush to make a tight deadline.

A week is a comfortable time in which to write a five-page report, but you may very well want five weeks for 25-page paper. The general rule is to start as soon as possible after the assignment is given. Okay, the speech is over. Let's get down to the task at hand.

STEP ONE: THINK

As always, in the first stage of the writing process, think before you act. For a research report, thinking consists of finding a topic, exploring possible research sources, doing your research, taking notes, and organizing your notes into an outline. That's a lot of thinking—and well worth every minute it takes.

Although some teachers will assign a specific topic ("Write five pages exploring scientific response to a recent supernova"), most teachers give you only a broad range of subject area ("Write five pages on a current issue in astronomy"). Your job is to find and focus a topic broad enough to be interesting, but narrow enough to be covered in the page limit assigned.

Make sure the topic you choose is one about which plenty of information is available!

Where do you get ideas for a topic? You can find suggestions back in chapter 5. Here are some additional approaches:

> ⌒◠╲╱╲╱◠ **POWER LINE** ◠◠╲╱╲◠⌒
>
> All my books literally come to me in the form of a sentence, an original sentence which contains the entire book.
>
> —Raymond Federman

- *For science:* Visit a science or natural history museum; read the science news in your local newspaper or take a look at *Omni, Nature, Scientific American,* or another popular science magazine; visit a planetarium; take a trip to a zoo or a botanical garden; skim the table of contents of your textbook.

- *For social studies/history/sociology:* Visit a history museum or historical society; read the newspaper or a journal of opinion such as *The Nation, The New Yorker, Commentary, The National Review, Atlantic*

Monthly, Harper's, or *The New Republic;* think back on your own
family history and personal experience; look through your textbook.

- *For English/literature/the arts:* Visit an art museum; attend a concert,
play, or opera; browse through art history books; read *Art in America*
or another magazine that focuses on art; read the book review and
arts sections in your area's newspaper; visit art and photography
exhibits.

- *For all topics:* Recall books, newspapers, and magazines that you have
already read; skim through your textbook and read over the table of
contents; remember current events that interest you; browse through
the library or the card catalog in the subject area that relates to your
assignment; freewrite on your assignment for five minutes.

After you choose a general topic, focus it. For example, Ed's psychology
professor has assigned a brief research paper exploring "a topic of your choice."

Ed turns to his personal interests to help him find a topic. Since Ed was a little
kid, his beloved dog, Marbles, has been an important part of his life. When Ed
went away to college, Marbles stayed behind with Ed's family, and Ed misses
him a lot. He decides to write about the relationship between pets and their
owners.

But, Ed realizes, this is an enormous subject. Here's how Ed's thinking goes as
he narrows his topic:

> I'd like to write about pets and their owners. Hmmm, why do owners
> keep pets? There must be lots of reasons—for a two-page paper, I'd better
> pick just one. "Owners keep pets because they're lonely?" Okay, that's
> not bad, but it's a little depressing. And it's still a little broad. Remember
> lonely old Mrs. Dershowitz? She was so skinny and pale, and she had that
> little white dog that looked just like her—that's it! Pets That Resemble Their
> Owners.

Before Ed starts to work on his paper, he should check his topic with his
teacher. This will ensure that he won't have to spend hours researching a topic
that is too narrow, too broad, or simply not acceptable for the assignment. Ed
discusses his idea with Professor Gomez, and she even suggests a key journal
article that he might read about his topic.

STEP TWO: ACT

Like Ed, once you have identified your topic, begin your quest for information:

- Use the card catalog to find books about your topic.
- Check the *Readers' Guide to Periodical Literature* for magazine articles related to your topic.
- Use the library computer.
- Check the indexes of journals in your field. Your teacher can usually recommend the major journals you should review.
- Ask the librarian for help. Most librarians love to help people find information, so why not take advantage of this wonderful, free, and helpful source?

Consider this phase of report-writing to be the exploration phase. Don't feel that you've wasted time if you haven't started writing anything, or even taken a book home from the library. If you come out of this phase with a list of useful sources, and if the list includes all the information about each of those sources that will let you find them easily, consider your exploration a success.

Explore Your Sources

Think of the first day you go to the library to begin your research as your exploration day. Don't read every word of every research source you find. If you do, you could be in still sitting in the library long after your report is due!

- In books, scan the index or the table of contents.
- In periodicals, skim articles, looking at section headings.

In both cases, decide whether to read the item at all, then choose which section, chapter, or page to read. Also, glance at footnotes and bibliographies for more research ideas. Sometimes they will lead you to your most useful sources.

In this exploratory stage of the research process, you might find that there is so much information on your topic that you could never cover it all. That is a sign that your topic is too broad and you need to narrow it. On the other hand, you might find that there simply isn't enough material on your topic. For a research paper, you really should use three different sources at the very least, so finding just one book or article would be a sign that your topic is too narrow. As a general rule, if you've checked your library's card catalog, the *Reader's Guide to Periodical Literature,* and several reference books related to your topic, and you cannot find at least five sources, your topic is too narrow and needs to be expanded or even changed.

As you explore, you will probably find some sources that you know will be helpful later. This is the time to start recording your sources so that you'll be able to find them again, and so that you'll have all the information you need to document them in your report. We recommend making *source cards,* or index cards with basic information about each source. Record the information on your source cards as follows:

- Author, last name first
  In this case, author had a title—Ph.D.
  et al. means "and others"; used when many people write an article
- Title of article
- Journal
- Journal number; could also be date
- Page numbers on which article appears
- Title of book
- Place of publication
- Publisher
- Date

Here's text from two of Ed's cards as an example:

Pool, Jean, Ph.D., et al., "Too Close for Comfort: Resemblances Between Pets and Their Human Companions in Scottsdale, Arizona," *Wind Chimes: A Review of Current Trends,* No. 64, pp. 99–105

Tels, Turr, *Pet "Ownership": The World of Animals and Their Humans,* New York: Anthropomorph Press, 1974

As he writes his source cards, Ed labels each one with a letter in red. That way, when he takes notes, he can label each note card with the letter of the matching source card. As his research progresses, he will make a new card for every book he uses.

Take Notes

As you begin your real research, take notes on index cards. We emphatically support this method for one simple reason—it works best. Rather than making our case for index cards now, we ask that you trust us. You will see just a little way down the line that index cards can make the difference between a report that gets written smoothly and easily and one that turns into the report from hell. Here are a few pointers to use when taking notes:

- Write only one fact per card. Even if you have lots of room left over, go to a new card for your next fact.

- Don't write down every word you read—summarize! And use abbreviations. Just be sure that you will be able to decipher your notes later!

- Put quotation marks around other people's words. If you want to quote just part of a sentence, put an ellipses (three dots) in place of the words you leave out.

- On each note card, note the source in which you found your information by writing in the upper right-hand corner the letter from the appropriate source card. Note the exact page number or numbers on which the information was found as well.

- This one is a little tricky, but perhaps most important of all: As you read, mentally divide your information into categories.

Ed, for example, finds that, at the beginning, his research breaks down into two main areas: general information on pets that look like their owners and theories on why pets resemble their owners. *The more he reads, the smaller categories his categories become;* for example, one of his original categories is "similarities between people and pets."

We Said "Take Notes," not "Make Copies"! It is a big temptation to copy from your source when you are taking notes. You don't mean to plagiarize—you just do not want to miss any important information. Don't yield to temptation! Use your head before your pencil. Think about what you are reading and writing, and get down the important ideas IN YOUR OWN WORDS.

As he reads, Ed breaks that down into two smaller categories: "similarities in body language," and "similarities in facial expressions." In the upper left-hand corner of each note card he writes a short phrase identifying the category; for example, "body language," and "facial expressions." The technical word for such a phrase is a *slug*. If you use the same method as Ed, when you organize your notes you'll be so glad that you'll be writing us thank-you notes and sending us flowers for making your life so much easier!

Just in case you want to get really fancy, you can color-code your note cards by making a colored dot in the upper left-hand corner of each card instead of naming the category. Here's a way Ed could have color-coded his cards:

I. General information on pets resembling owners (green)

A. humorous (green plus blue)

B. serious (green plus yellow)

II. Theories on why pets resemble owners (red)

A. insecure owners choose similar pets (red plus pink)

B. pets/owners change in appearance over time (red plus purple)

Most teachers will want you to use at least three sources for your research. If your paper is fairly long (more than eight pages) five or more is better. You will know you are finished with your research when you start finding only information you've already noted. (You may want cards from different sources that contain the same information. It makes a better case for a hard-to-believe fact if you can cite two sources that back it up.)

Organize Your Notes

Now you will see why we are so intense about using index cards. They can be moved around.

- Sit at a large table or on the floor and sort the cards so that those with the same or similar slugs, or the same color coding, are piled together; then go through each pile, putting the cards in an order that makes sense. Order of importance will probably work best.

- Read over your notes as you sort. At some point, you'll probably trash a few of your cards. Don't feel obliged to include information just because you have it; use only the information that directly relates to your thesis.

- Keep sorting until your notes start to "tell a story." At that point you'll find that they read almost like a finished paper, and all you need to add are your own ideas and, of course, transitions to help the reader get from one idea to another.

- When you are pretty sure you have your cards in the best order, number them. Use rubber bands or paper clips to hold together the cards you think will make one paragraph.

NOTE: If your sources are all books that can be checked out of the library and taken home, or if you have a laptop to use in the library, you can take your notes on a computer. Make "source cards" and "note cards" just as we have described. The computer gives you the same flexibility that you get from index card—you can easily reorganize your information and move it around.

Make an Outline

Your next organizational task is to turn your notes into a formal outline. On your outline, don't copy all your notes—just use a few words to remind you of the information on each card. If some of your information just doesn't seem to fit, ask yourself: Is it really important? If not, perhaps it should be trashed. If the information is important, you may have to do a little reorganizing to fit it in. It is also possible that you will pick up on some gaps in your outline, which may mean an important piece of information is missing. In that case, it might mean you go back to the books or the library for a little additional research. Remember to refer to chapter 11 for detailed instructions on outlining.

Take your time with your outline, because, although you may not stick to every detail, it is truly the backbone of your report. With a well-organized outline, when you are drafting, you will already know what information to include in each paragraph. That means you can concentrate less on *what* to write, and more on *how* you present your information. You will come out with a nice tight draft that will go into the repair stage in pretty good shape to begin with.

When Ed begins his outline he has already color-coded and organized his index cards, so he knows where in the outline they should fall. Here is the working outline that will show him exactly what information to use and where. Notice he refers to some of his cards by number. You can jump ahead and compare Ed's outline to his rough draft, if you wish.

Pets Resembling Their Owners

Thesis Statement: Many owners seem to resemble their pets, but no one is quite sure why.

I. General overview of topic

    A. Humorous examples

        1. Katz, *New Yorker*, card 3

        2. P. King Eese, *Laff Riot*, card 11

    B. Serious studies

        1. Per Akeet's groundbreaking research

        2. Moss Kito's study

II. Theories on why pets resemble owners

    A. Jean Pool: because owners are insecure

    B. X. Q. Smee: because animals/owners change

III. Conclusion

    A. Smee has been both challenged and supported.

    B. More work still to be done

    C. Cite Akeet, quote, card 14

STEP THREE: REPAIR

Drafting

When it comes to drafting, use your outline, but don't "marry" it; be open to new approaches and ideas as they come to you.

Also, *leave yourself time*. Writing a 25-page paper in one all-nighter is not the recommended method. (However, if tomorrow's date on your calendar says "Report due," this little sermon won't help you. Just grit your teeth and move on. We'll be right behind you.)

⌐ⱮⱲ○ **POWER LINE** ○ⱮⱲⱭ

I start early in the morning. I'm usually out in the woods with the dog as soon as it gets light; then I drink a whole lot of tea and start as early as I can, and I go as long as I can.

—Robert Stone

- **Beginning, middle, and end.** Many people like to write the introduction first because it helps them focus their thinking; on the other hand, others like to draft their introductions last, because then they can give a better overview and know exactly how to preview what is to come. Either way, when you do write your introduction, use a question, startling fact, or clear thesis statement to pull the reader in. When you come to write the body of your paper, stick closely to your outline. Make sure that each point relates to your thesis statement. For your conclusion, end with a quote, a question, or some other strong statement that points readers towards the significance of what you've written.

- **Unity, completeness, coherence.** If you have organized your notes and written a good, tight outline, you have probably built these three good things into your draft. As you draft, pay particular attention to coherence. Make sure all your information is in a logical order that flows smoothly and makes sense. Remind yourself that each paragraph should focus on one main idea, and that the main idea should be expressed in a topic sentence, with other sentences supporting it. And keep transitions in mind to guide readers from one thought to another.

- **Heads.** Flip through the pages of this book to see how we've used heads to label parts of the book that contain several paragraphs on whole categories of information. For example, this paragraph comes under the head, "Repair." Ed could use the head, "Serious Studies," and write a paragraph describing each study. Find some typographic way of distinguishing heads from the rest of your report. If you are working on a computer, you can use boldface or italics. If not, just underline your heads.

A Word about Heads. If you like, your heads can follow your outline. Say your paragraphs are based on the capital letters. you could use each Roman-numeral idea as a head. Or, say your paragraphs are based on the Arabic-numeral ideas. You could then use the capital letter ideas as heads.

- **Documentation.** Always use your own words unless you are quoting directly. In that case, enclose the quoted words in quotation marks and use a footnote to tell where you got the quote and who wrote it.

A Word about Documentation. Using other people's words outside of a direct quote is considered plagiarism. If you get caught—and there's a very good chance that you will—you are likely to fail your course. You might even be suspended or expelled from school.

Even when you are using your own words, you must *document* a source when you are presenting someone else's *original idea* or reporting information that is not *common knowledge*. By common knowledge, we mean something most people know in the first place. For example, if you state in your paper that "many people enjoy keeping pets," you don't have to document that fact, even if you read it in a book. Everyone knows that lots of people have pets. However, if you state that "60 percent of the population in Katzendogs, West Virginia, own pets," you will have to tell where you found that information.

How do you document your information? By writing footnotes and a bibliography.

- *Footnotes* are those little numbered notes that appear at the bottom of a page and tell the name of the source a fact came from. Each fact that will be footnoted is marked with a number, and the footnote is marked with the same number. Most teachers will accept a page of footnotes at the end of your report (which is easier to type) rather than insisting that footnotes appear at the bottom of each page.

- A *bibliography* is a list of all the books from which you actually used information. It will appear at the very end of your report. Now you see why it is so important to make source cards, give each one a letter, and label note cards with matching letters.

Different teachers sometimes prefer different styles for footnotes and bibliographies. If your teacher hasn't explained exactly how these should be styled, find a style sheet, book, or pamphlet that tells exactly how to cite different types of sources.

Some widely accepted styles can be found in:

> *MLA Style Sheet* (published by the Modern Language Association)
>
> *Chicago Manual of Style* (published by the University of Chicago Press)
>
> *Words into Type* (published by Prentice Hall)

You don't have to do formal footnoting or referencing in a rough draft, but do indicate each place that a footnote or reference is needed. (To see how to do this, look ahead at Ed's rough draft.) Then put in the full footnote when you revise.

Revising and Editing

Take a break! Even if you don't have time for a whole day or night away from your report, take a little break. Then go back to your report refreshed for the last phase of the writing process—the phase that will result in a final, polished draft. The thing that's finished. The thing you don't have to work on any more. And the thing you will be proud to hand in to your teacher.

- **Two Reads.** We advise you to read through your paper at least twice.
- **The First Time.** Make a few notes, but try not to stop for lengthy corrections. You might use those little sticky flags to remind you to come back to any problem spots in your draft. As you read, check for unity, completeness, and coherence. Ask yourself if any irrelevant information has somehow crept into your draft; if any information is missing; if your ideas are clear and in a logical order; and if your information is flowing smoothly.

- **The Second Time.** Correct issues as you find them. For example, as you move from paragraph to paragraph, can you add transition words or sentences to clarify the connections between ideas? Does each paragraph focus on one main idea, expressed in a topic sentence? Can you improve your style by combining short sentences or breaking up long ones? Could you choose more specific, vivid, or stronger words? Go back to chapter 16 on making repairs and review what you can do to make your draft the best it can be.

- **Complete Your Documentation.** Now is the time to get your footnotes and bibliography into shape. These are the final finishing touches you'll give to your report.

- **Write Footnotes.** First, make sure you have identified each place a footnote is needed. If you missed anything, identify it now. Then write the footnotes, making sure to use your teacher's style guidelines or one of the generally accepted style sheets. Is each quote enclosed in quotation marks?

- **Write a Bibliography.** A bibliography is a list of the sources you used. It generally includes both works you have footnoted and works you simply read. However, if you think that a work wasn't very useful, and if you haven't cited from it, you can leave it out. Start by getting out your source cards and putting them in alphabetical order by author's last name. Set aside the ones you are not planning to include in your bibliography. To see how a bibliography should be organized and formatted, take a look at the end of Ed's final draft.

Finally, give your report one last read, using the following checklist to make sure you haven't missed anything in the repair process.

Research Report Checklist

- Have I written a good introduction that will draw readers into my report?
- Is my thesis statement clearly stated?
- Does my report reflect the "three good things": unity, completeness, and coherence?
- Have I documented every new piece of information I got from my sources?

- Have I enclosed all quotations in quotation marks and documented them?
- Except for quotations, have I used my own words throughout my report?
- Does my conclusion sum up my main ideas and give my readers something to remember or think about?
- Have I used the proper form for footnotes, either at the bottom of each page or at the end of my report?
- Have I included a bibliography in the proper form?

Plug In

Here are the rough and final drafts of Ed's research paper on why pets resemble their owners. Get out your red pen and mark up Ed's rough draft as you see fit. Then compare your work to ours as you look at the final drafts. (You will notice that Ed's report is shorter than most. We kept it that way on purpose so you wouldn't have to wade through 25 pages about Ed's topic . . . and so this book wouldn't be about 100 pages too long!)

A Brief Survey of How Pets Resemble Their Owners

Many people have noted the resemblance between pets who look like their owners. But is there a scientific basis for this theory? Although scientists are still slugging it out over this issue, many scientists—not cranks, but people with good reputations—have noted a resemblance between pets and their owners.

Dr. Per Akeet, for example, found that of the 150 pet owners whom he studied, 78 percent owned animals who could be said to resemble them in at least one of the three major appearance factors that he identified. (FOOTNOTE—Source Card A) Dr. Moss Kito published a report detailing similarities between married pet owners, whom Dr. Kito found didn't only look like their pets but also looked a lot like each other. (FOOTNOTE–Source Card F).

But why? Did owners choose pets who actually did in fact resemble them, in a weird, twisted attempt to assert their own identities, to see themselves mirrored in a pet that they owned? Yes, said Jean Pool, Ph.D. Pool took a team of researchers and she conducted an in-depth study of 12 subjects in Scottsdale. They all owned pets very similar to themselves. They were so similar that Pool said, "Many of their neighbors and even family members could not tell them apart." (FOOTNOTE–Source Card D, Note Card 55 for quotation page number) Pool said that the owners were habitually insecure all the time and required a very great deal of reinforcement from the external world. Therefore, as a result, these owners had literally chosen pets to remind them "who . . . they were." (FOOTNOTE–Source Card D, Note Card 57)

Another theory has been put forward by X. Q. Smee, Ph.D. Smee graphed the progressive resemblance between 42 animals and their owners whom he studied in Stockholm, Sweden. He found that in the first year of ownership, pets and owners averaged only a 15 percent degree of resemblance (using Smee's own "Pet-Owner Look-Alike Scale"). Smee contends that in a slow but inexorable process of mutual influence, pets and owners come to resemble each other. This is how he explains it: when the owner originally acquired the pet, the two may have been quite different in appearance and the way they looked. However, by the time that animal and human had co-habited for three years, they had acquired many similar physical characteristics. By the second year, average resemblance had increased to 40 percent. At the end of the third year, average resemblance had further risen to a remarkable 73 percent. (THERE'S A FOOTNOTE IN HERE SOMEWHERE–SOURCE CARD H–BUT WHERE???)

Smee's findings have been challenged by numerous scientists since they were first published in 1992, but many more scientists have come forward to support his work. (ONE FOOTNOTE FOR BOTH CHALLENGERS AND SUPPORTERS? OR TWO SEPARATE FOOTNOTES? CHECK CARDS!!) Unfortunately, the issue remains unresolved. Dr. Akeet, however, has these encouraging words to say:

As long as people and animals live together, our relationships will continue to fascinate us. And as long as people are fascinated, we may expect them to conduct scientific research. Sooner or later, we will have the knowledge we seek–and our pets will be all the happier for it.

Plug In Solution

My Dog, Myself:
Studies of Resemblance Between Pets and Their Owners

Many authors have humorously noted the resemblance between pets and their owners.[1] But is there a scientific basis for this notion? Although there is still a great deal of controversy about this issue in scientific circles, many reputable scientists have in fact noted a resemblance between pets and their owners.

The renowned Norwegian animal psychologist, Dr. Per Akeet, for example, found that of the 150 pet owners whom he studied, 78 percent owned animals who could be said to resemble them in at least one of the three major appearance factors that he identified (height, weight, and coloring).² Likewise, Dr. Moss Kito published a groundbreaking report detailing similarities between married pet owners, whom Dr. Kito found to resemble not only their pets but also each other.³

These studies are well known. The question that had not been answered, however, was *why*. Did owners choose pets who in fact resembled them, in a bizarre attempt to assert their own identities, to see themselves mirrored in an animal companion? This was the assertion of Jean Pool, Ph.D., who, with a team of researchers, conducted an in-depth study of 12 subjects in Scottsdale, Arizona, all of whom owned pets so similar to themselves in appearance that, as Pool put it, "Many of their neighbors and even family members could not tell them apart."⁴ According to Pool, the owners, habitually insecure and requiring a great deal of reinforcement from the external world, had literally chosen pets to remind them "who . . . they were."⁵

An alternative theory has been put forward by X. Q. Smee, Ph.D. Smee contends that in a slow but inexorable process of mutual influence, pets and owners come to resemble each other. In other words, when the owner originally acquired the pet, the two may have been quite different in appearance. However, by the time that animal and human had co-habited for three years, they had acquired many similar physical characteristics. To demonstrate this startling contention, Smee graphed the progressive resemblance between 42 animals and their owners, whom he studied in Stockholm, Sweden. He found that in the first year of ownership, pets and owners averaged a 15 percent degree of resemblance (using Smee's "Pet Owner LookAlike Scale"). By the second year, average resemblance had increased to 40 percent. At the end of the third year, average resemblance had further risen to a remarkable 73 percent.⁶

Smee's findings have been challenged by numerous scientists since they were first published in 1992,⁷ but many more scientists have come forward to support his work.⁸ Unfortunately, the issue remains unresolved. Dr. Akeet, however, "grandfather" of animal-resemblance research, has these encouraging words to say:

As long as people and animals live together, their relationships will continue to fascinate us. And as long as people are fascinated, we may expect them to conduct scientific research. Sooner or later, we will have the knowledge we seek, and our pets will be all the happier for it.

Notes

[1] See for example Kitty Katz, "Why Do Pets Look So Darn Much Like Their Owners?" *New Yorker*, June 5, 1955, pp. 10–15, and P. King Eese, "Annoying Little Dogs and Their Annoying Little Owners," *Laff Riot*, Spring 1990, pp. 322–323.

[2] Dr. Per Akeet, "Measuring the Resemblance Between Pets and Their Owners on the Three-Point Per Akeet Scale," published in *Animal Studies* (New York: Food Chain Books, 1980), pp. 40–49.

[3] Dr. Moss Kito, "Married Couples and Animal Companions," in *The Journal of Trivial But Interesting Studies*, Fall 1975, pp. 66–75.

[4] Jean Pool, Ph.D., et al., "Too Close for Comfort: Resemblances Between Pets and Their Human Companions in Scottsdale, Arizona," in *Wind Chimes: A Review of Current Trends*, No. 64, p. 99.

[5] Ibid., p. 102.

[6] X. Q. Smee, "Why Do They Look So Alike?: Human-Animal Congruence in the Scandinavian Regions," in *Bulldogs Monthly*, June 1992, p. 76.

[7] See for example Jack Russell, Scott Tee, et al., "Terriers or Toddlers: The Confusion Between Children and Pets in X. Q. Smee's Study of Pet Ownership," in *Wait a Minute: A Review of Rebuttals*, Spring 1993, pp. 56–65, and Jean Pool, Ph.D., et al., "I Don't Believe It: A Refutation of X. Q. Smee's Refutation of Me," also in *Wait a Minute*, Fall 1993, pp. 74–79.

[8] See for example *Controversies: A Scientific Review*, whose entire May 1994 issue is devoted to articles supporting Smee's work.

Bibliography

Books

Akeet, Dr. Per, "Measuring the Resemblance Between Pets and Their Owners on the Three-Point Per Akeet Scale," published in *Animal Studies*, New York: Food Chain Books, 1980: pp. 40–49.

Pets, People, and Places in Pittsburgh: A Memoir, Cambridge: Cambridge University Press, 1997.

Tels, Turr, *Pet "Ownership": The World of Animals and Their Humans*, New York: Anthropomorph Press, 1974.

Journals

"The Smee Issue," *Controversies: A Scientific Review*, May 1994: 1–140.

Eese, P. King, "Annoying Little Dogs and Their Annoying Little Owners," *Laff Riot*, Spring 1990: 322-323.

Katz, Kitty, "Why Do Pets Look So Darn Much Like Their Owners?" *The New Yorker*, June 5, 1955: 10–15.

Kito, Dr. Moss, "Married Couples and Animal Companions," *The Journal of Trivial But Interesting Studies*, Fall 1975: 66–75.

Pool, Jean, Ph.D. et al., "I Don't Believe It: A Refutation of X. Q. Smee's Refutation of Me," *Wait A Minute: A Review of Rebuttals*, Fall 1993, pp. 74–79.

"Too Close for Comfort: Resemblances Between Pets and Their Human Companions in Scottsdale, Arizona," *Wind Chimes: A Review of Current Trends*, No. 64: 99–103.

Russell, Jack, Scott Tee, et. al., "Terriers or Toddlers: The Confusion Between Children and Pets in X. Q. Smee's Study of Pet Ownership" *Wait a Minute: A Review of Rebuttals*, Spring 1993: pp. 56–65.

Smee, X. Q., "Why Do They Look So Alike?: Human-Animal Congruence in the Scandinavian Regions," *Bulldogs Monthly*, June 1992: 73–80.

Encyclopedias

"Pets." *Encyclopedia Vulcanica*. 1994 ed.

Interviews

Russell, Jack. Personal interview. 23 March 1997.

○ Now You Have the Power

Congratulations! You have made it through the writing process, or should we say you've *waded* through the writing process. You have seen a number of ways that this process can be applied: to writing for school, to real-life writing, to writing on the job.

> **∿ POWER LINE ∿**
>
> Writing is the hardest work in the world not involving heavy lifting.
>
> —Pete Hamill

You have lots of practice using the written word for a variety of purposes: to communicate your ideas, to persuade people to agree with you, to apply for admission to a college, to apply for a job.

But if we've done our job and the true purpose of this book has been fulfilled, what you have gained most of all is the self-confidence to express yourself in writing in the many situations in life where writing is required. Even if you have to do a type of writing that we haven't covered, you have everything you need to do it right, because all writing follows essentially the same process.

Our final gift to you is the following question-and-answer chart. No matter what you have to write, whether it's a short note to your third-grader's teacher or a 50-page report, it will be there for you. Apply the questions to what you are writing, and the answers will lead you in the right direction.

THINK

What is my purpose?

Who is my audience?

What can I do to fulfill my purpose with this audience?

ACT

How should I get my audience's attention?

What is my main idea?

What are some details–evidence, facts, examples, anecdotes–that I can use to support that idea?

How can I drive my point home at the end?

REPAIR

Have I really fulfilled my purpose?

Is there anything else that this audience needs or wants to know?

Have I varied my sentences?

Have I chosen my words carefully?

Is my writing unified, complete, and coherent?

Have I corrected all errors in spelling, grammar, and punctuation?

Add to your chart these words of wisdom. We know you've heard them before, but one more time won't hurt: Although different types of writing require different approaches, the structure almost always stays the same:

- *Introduction*: How do I grab my readers' attention?
- *Body*: How do I support my main idea?
- *Conclusion*: How do I reinforce my main idea and give readers some sense of why it matters?

That's it! Now you have the basics of writing power at your command. Remember that if you ever again feel the old heart doing a nose dive when you hear the words, "Write a _____." And please revisit the

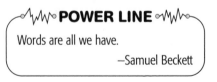

POWER LINE

Words are all we have.

–Samuel Beckett

pages of this book for a little refresher course or confidence boost any time you feel the need. You can always get a little help from your friends.

Want more information about our services, products or the nearest Kaplan center?

1 **Call our nationwide toll-free numbers:**

1-800-KAP-TEST for information on our test prep courses, private tutoring and admissions consulting

1-800-KAP-ITEM for information on our books and software

2 **Connect with us online:**

On the web, go to:
www.kaptest.com

3 **Write to:**

Kaplan
888 Seventh Avenue
New York, NY 10106

KAPLAN